The Latin Bass Book:
A Practical Guide

by Oscar Stagnaro
(bassist with Paquito D'Rivera and Professor at Berklee College of Music)

and Chuck Sher
(author of "The Improvisor's Bass Method")

Contributing Editor – Dave Belove
(bassist with Rebeca Mauleón's "Round Trip", "The Machete Ensemble", etc.)

Includes 3 Play-Along CDs, featuring
Oscar Stagnaro - bass
Rebeca Mauleón - keyboards, vocals
Orestes Vilató - percussion, vocals
Edgardo Cambón - percussion, vocals
Carlos Caro - percussion, vocals
Mark Walker - drums
Dario Eskenazi - keyboards
and more.

D1611578

Editor - Chuck Sher
Musical Editors - Larry Dunlap, Oscar Stagnaro and Rebeca Mauleón
Cover Artwork - Michelle White, San Francisco, CA
Cover Design - Attila Nagy, Cotati, CA
CDs mastered by Fred Catero, Catero Productions, San Carlos, CA
Music Copying - Chuck Gee, San Francisco
©2001 Sher Music Co., P.O.Box 445, Petaluma, CA 94953.
ISBN 1-883217-11-3

Notes About the Enclosed Play-Along CDs

The accompanying CDs to "The Latin Bass Book" were designed to provide:
a) audio illustrations of how each exercise should be played, and also
b) years of professional-level play-along accompaniment.

How To Best Utilize These CDs - Please read!

1) Go through each exercise and listen to how the bass part fits in with the rest of the rhythm section while you watch the transcription go by.

2) Then try playing what is written yourself until you sound pretty much like the bass on the CD.

3) You can then turn off the bass channel and play along with the rhythm track yourself, improvising your own lines based on the material presented in that exercise—especially any rhythms written out at the end of the transcription of Oscar's bass line.

4) After you've gone through the whole book in this way, you can then use the CDs to practice anything you want, not just the initial rhythms suggested for that track.

We hope you will find these CDs invaluable in giving you professional Latin rhythm sections to play along with. Enjoy!

PERSONNEL:

Afro-Cuban Exercises
CD One - All tracks; CD Two - Tracks 1-15; CD Three - Tracks 8 & 18
Oscar Stagnaro - bass
Rebeca Mauleón - keyboards, vocals
Orestes Vilató - percussion, vocals
Edgardo Cambón - percussion, vocals
Carlos Caro - percussion, vocals
Recorded and mixed by Oscar Autie at O Studios, El Cerrito, CA

Brazilian and Caribbean Exercises
CD Two - Tracks 16-23; CD Three - Tracks 1-7
Oscar Stagnaro - bass
Dario Eskenazi - keyboards
Attila Nagy - keyboards (Track 7 only)
Mark Walker - drums
Pernell Sarturnino - percussion
Recorded at Alleycat Studio by John Lee, South Orange, NJ.
Mixed at ArtDrums Studio by Alberto Netto, Arlington, MA

South American Exercises
CD Three - Tracks 9-17
Oscar Stagnaro - bass
Aquiles Baez - Venezuelan cuatro (Tracks 9-13) and guitar (Tracks 16-17)
Omar Ledezma - congas and percussion (Tracks 9-13)
Franco Pinna - drums (Tracks 14-15)
Julio Santillan - guitar (Tracks 14-15)
Martin Zarzar - cajon (Tracks 16-17)
Jorge Perez Albela - hand claps (Tracks 6-17)
DPelot - quijada, guiro & bells (Tracks 16-17)
Recorded and Mixed at ArtDrums Studio by Alberto Netto, Arlington, MA

All CDs mastered by "The Master", Fred Catero, at Catero Productions, San Carlos, CA

Editor's Foreword

The role of the bass in Latin music is primarily to hold down the rhythmic and harmonic foundation of the tune. To the casual listener there is certainly a lot of repetition in most Latin bass lines. But if you listen closely you'll usually find a myriad of subtle variations that give the music an extra kick without destroying the underlying groove. This book will show you how that is done.

"The Latin Bass Book" contains the most comprehensive study ever published of the main Afro-Cuban and Brazilian styles of bass playing, as well as shorter sections on other Caribbean and Latin American styles and also Latin jazz bass playing.

If you go through the book and faithfully follow the written instructions, you will be in possession of all the information you need to fulfill your function in a Latin or Latin jazz rhythm section. This is a practical guide for the motivated student to learn how to play in various Latin idioms, not an historical accounting of how these idioms developed. For that, please see Sher Music Co.'s "The True Cuban Bass" by Carlos Del Puerto and Silvio Vergara, an invaluable document.

Much thanks goes to Attila Nagy for designing the cover, as well as his informative contribution to the reggae section of the book; Michelle White for the beautiful cover art work; Larry Dunlap and Rebeca Mauleón for their world-class transcriptions; all the wonderful rhythm section players on the CDs; Dave Belove for contributing Chapter Four, on the bass' relation to clave; Chuck Gee for the easy-to-read music manuscript; Fred Catero for a masterful mastering job; the talented photographers who contributed to this book; Andy Gonzalez and Pedro Perez who allowed us to include transcriptions of some of their recorded bass lines; and lastly Oscar Stagnaro, who makes this book come alive with such grace and soul.

As the world gets closer together, having a working knowledge of Latin bass playing will increasingly be a prerequisite for any professional, improvising bassist. This book is designed to help you learn to play this passionate and beautiful music. Enjoy the ride! - **Chuck Sher**

About Oscar Stagnaro

Bassist Oscar Stagnaro, originally from Peru, studied at the Conservatory of Music in Lima, Peru and worked extensively doing studio work and live performances with many international artists and local bands before moving to the USA in 1979. Since then he has been a very active performer and one of the most versatile bass players on the East Coast. His mastery of different styles including jazz, fusion, Latin jazz, Brazilian jazz and South American music has helped him to travel the world performing with the very best Latin jazz artists.

Mr. Stagnaro has been an Associate Professor at Berklee College of Music since 1988, where he teaches private lessons, workshops and ensembles, and has represented Berklee at the IAJE Conventions since 1997. He is an active clinician and has given clinics on bass playing in Peru, Puerto Rico, Cosa Rica, Venezuela, Germany, Spain and the USA.

Mr. Stagnaro has recorded with Paquito D'Rivera, the United Nations Orchestra, Dave Valentin, Charlie Sepulveda, The Caribbean Jazz Project and many others (see Discography on page 262.) He has also played with Chucho Valdés, Michel Camilo, Dave Liebman, Ray Barretto, Mark Murphy, Tom Harrell, Leny Andrade, Claudio Roditi, Danilo Perez, Tiger Okashi, Bob Moses, Bob Mintzer, Steve Kuhn, Nestor Torres and many others. His first CD under his own name, "Mariella's Dream", is on the Songosaurus label and features Paquito D'Rivera, Dave Samuels, Ed Simon, Alex Acuña and Ramón Stagnaro.

Mr. Stagnaro endorses Etifani speakers, Fender strings and Guild and Warwick basses.

A Note From Oscar

This work is dedicated to my Father, Rogelio, for his love and dedication; my wife Teresa for her love, comprehension, inspiration and huge patience; my children Paulo and Mariella who help me to find the meaning of life; to my brother Ramon, my first bass teacher; and to my best friend Pocho Purizaga. Thanks also to Paquito D'Rivera, Danilo Perez, the Pelots, my Boss at Berklee, Rich Appleman, Pedro Aiscorbe, Carlos Hayre, Aquiles Baez, Los Changos, Sal Cuevas, Alon Yavnai, Dave Valentin, Brenda Feliciano, Alberto Netto, Alain Malett, Lincoln Goines, Milton Cardona, Andy Narell, Dave Samuels, Victor Mendoza, Coc Salazar, Pancho Saenz and all my friends and collegues whom I have learned from and share the universal language of music.

CD One

CD Two and CD Three are on the inside back cover.

CD One
TRACK #1

Tuning Notes.

Note 1: To make the bass louder or softer (or to eliminate it altogether for play-along purposes), please use the Balance control on your stereo.

Note 2: The Sher Music publication "Muy Caliente!" uses selected tracks from the CDs in this book, so if you own "The Latin Bass Book" there is no need to buy "Muy Caliente!". If you already own "Muy Caliente!", you will be happy to find that this book contains transcriptions of every note Oscar Stagnaro plays there, plus lots more.

SECTION ONE - THE TUMBAO BASS LINE

CHAPTER ONE - *The Basic Tumbao and its Main Variations*

The simplest version of the most basic Afro-Cuban bass line, the tumbao, is as follows:

      Practice this rhythm along with Track #2 until each note is played with rhythmic authority. You might try accenting one of the beats in each bar for a while, then a different one (e.g. first the "1", then the "and of two", then the "4", etc.) This track uses mostly roots and fifths in the bass so you can focus completely on rhythmic accuracy. Here, and throughout the book, we have transcribed Oscar's playing on the accompanying CDs for you to study and play along with. After doing that, however, we strongly suggest that you improvise your own lines using the basic ideas and rhythms being presented.

> **CD One**
> **TRACK #2**

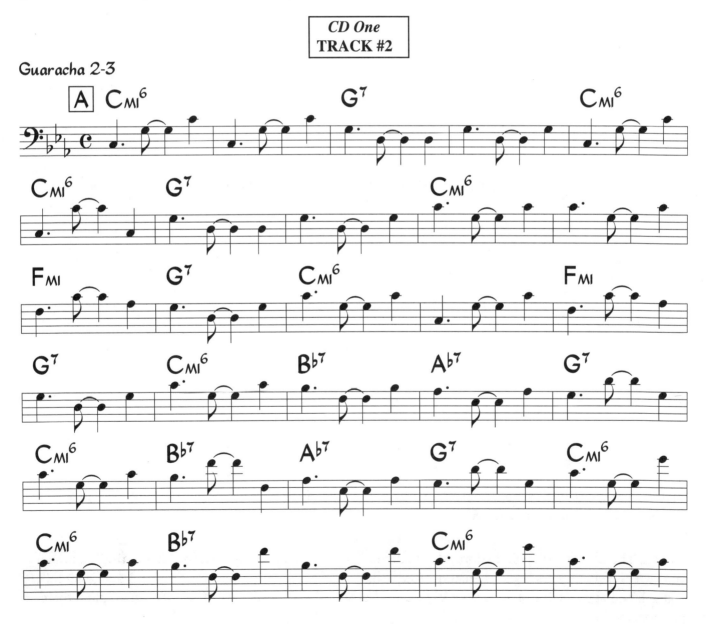

2

3

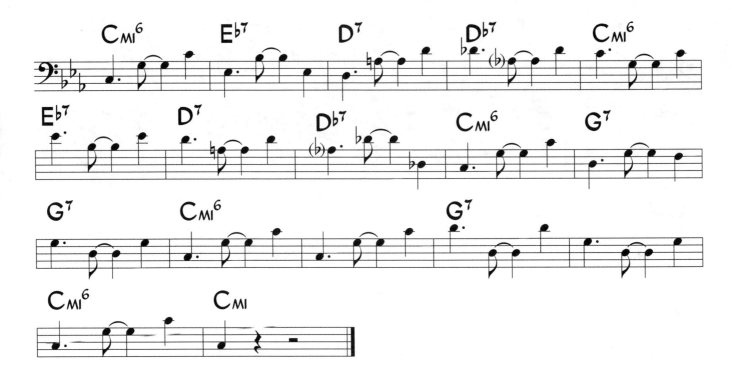

Edgardo Cambón, Orestes Vilató, Rebeca Mauleón, Carlos Caro, Oscar Stagnaro

5   This next track takes the one bar rhythm we just learned and adds different rhythms in the following bar to create some two bar patterns. After trying to match what Oscar plays here, we strongly suggest that you turn off the bass channel, and then play one phrase at a time (listed at the end of the transcription) along with this track until it feels natural to you. These phrases will prepare you to play the syncopated version of the tumbao later in the chapter.

**CD One
TRACK #3**

Here are the variations that Oscar uses on this track. Try using them one at a time when you improvise your own bass line on this exercise.

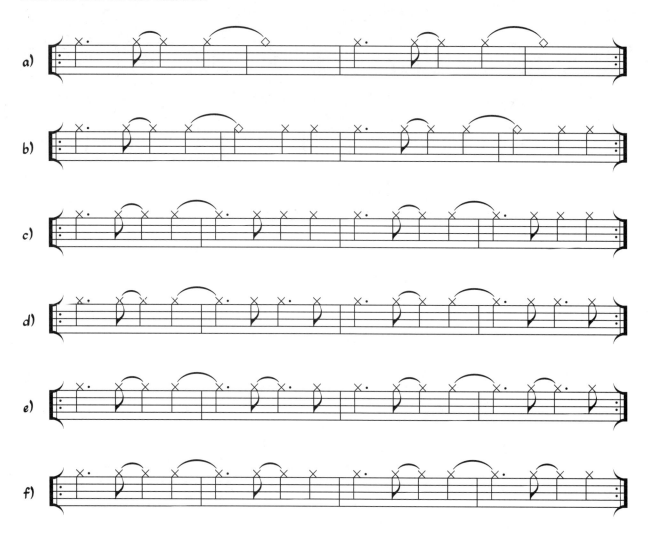

Oscar Stagnaro

Photo by Ken Franckling

9   The following figure is the same as the basic tumbao figure except that the "4" is tied to the "1" of the next bar. This syncopated version of the tumbao is the basic rhythm now in use for most Afro-Cuban bass lines—for such styles as the guaguanco, guaracha, rumba, mambo, bomba, son-montuno, etc. Please see "The True Cuban Bass" by Carlos Del Puerto and Silvio Vergara (published by Sher Music Co.) for an invaluable look at the historical evolution of each of these styles.

Practice this rhythm until you can play it in your sleep, until you can hear it inside you like your heartbeat. At least half of all bass lines played in Salsa are composed of nothing but this rhythm, with short variations (discussed later in this section of the book) but always returning to this basic tumbao pattern. The primary focus here should be on getting the rhythm to feel natural. Hint: Even though the "1" is not being played, you must be able to feel where it is every bar.

11

To help anchor the rhythmic aspect of your playing, try counting "1, 2 and, 3, 4" every bar (accenting the beats that you are actually playing in your line) until it is engrained in your subconscious. To help you feel how the basic tumbao rhythm fits against a steady pulse, first try playing along with the previous track and tapping your foot on 1 and 3. Then try tapping your foot on 2 and 4 instead. This has the advantage of getting you to feel beat 4 as one of the downbeats of 2 & 4, instead of it being an anticipation of beat 1 of the next bar.

13

Here is a typical salsa chord progression, transposed to different keys, that uses the tumbao bass line. Here only roots are used and the rhythm is played with virtually no variation (but it swings!). Try to imitate Oscar's sense of forward motion and complete rhythmic assurance, even after you turn off the bass track and are on your own.

CD One
TRACK #5

Med. Son-Pachanga ♩ = 156
(Perc. intro)

15

This next example uses some chord notes other than the roots and fifths, generally as leading tones to the next root. The time feel is still the most important element. If this transcription is too advanced for you to read at this point, just play the standard tumbao along with the CD track. We will study the rhythmic variations later.

17

19

Following are the basic variations of the tumbao that are found in standard dance-oriented salsa.

VARIATION 1  **or**

The first figure above is like the unsyncopated tumbao but the "and of 2" is not tied to the "3". This is often found in older styles of Cuban bass playing. The second version above is also the original bass rhythm for the mambo.

CD One
TRACK #7

Med. Charanga

20

VARIATION 2

This is the same as Variation #1 except that here the "4" is tied over to the "1" of the next bar. This is like the standard syncopated tumbao but adding the note on beat 3, creating a bass line with a little more rhythmic punch.

CD One
TRACK #8

Guaracha 3-2

23

Here the "3" is played instead of the "and of 2". This can create a nice contrast to the standard tumbao for particular sections of a tune. It is also used as the basic groove in a lot of older Cuban styles of bass playing.

**CD One
TRACK #9**

27

Andy Gonzalez

Photo by Jeffrey Kliman

VARIATION 4  (and variations of it listed on p. 32)

These are variations of one of the basic cha-cha-chá grooves but they are also used in son-montunos, guarachas, etc. They are presented here as a repeated rhythm but they are most often used as a temporary variation from a standard tumbao.

31

Here are some of the variations that Oscar uses on this track. Try using them one at a time, along with a regular tumbao, when you improvise your own bass line on this exercise.

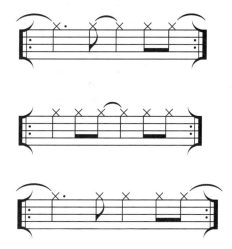

33

VARIATION 5

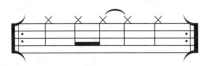

This is the rhythm of the typical guaracha bass line and is often intermingled with the standard tumbao in other styles as well (see Chapter 2 for more on this). The presence of the "2" in this bass line creates a unique feel, but the "and of 2" is usually the more strongly accented of the two notes.

Here are some of the variations that Oscar uses on this track. Try using them one at a time, along with a regular tumbao, when you improvise your own bass line on this exercise.

CHAPTER TWO - Combinations

By combining the variations in Chapter 1 with each other, a great variety of bass lines can be created that all spring from, and can support, a basic tumbao groove.

Here are some two bar phrases to learn, combining a bar of tumbao with a bar of one of the variations. After listening to the entire track, you should play each two bar phrase over and over, along with the rhythm section, until it feels natural and strong.

CD One TRACK #12

Guaracha 2-3 (Mozambique Intro/Outro)

(w/ piano, clave & güiro)   N.C.

(Mozambique 2-3)

(Guaracha 2-3)

39

41

This next track will again show how each variation in Chapter 1 can be integrated into a standard tumbao bass line. After listening to Oscar play these variations, we strongly recommend that you **write down the rhythm of each four bar phrase, one at a time, and then play it through the entire exercise**. This way they will become thoroughly engrained in your playing. The extra time you spend on this exercise will be invaluable in preparing you to play Afro-Cuban music with others. Don't skimp - repetition is the key to Latin bass playing! (Note: There are, of course, numerous other four bar phrases you could, and should, construct integrating these variations and the tumbao. Try singing a bass line to yourself and then write down the rhythm and practice it along with the CD track.)

43   Here you will find all the variations in Chapter One combined with the tumbao bass line, in this case, the unsyncopated version of the tumbao. Again, after playing through what is written here, try making up your own lines using this idea.

**CD One
TRACK #14**

Guaracha 2-3

Here is a second example of all the variations integrated within a tumbao groove. Again, you should write out the rhythm of any four-bar phrase shown here and play it through the entire exercise.

If you go no further than this chapter, but really make the rhythmic figures already presented an integral part of your playing, you will be able to fulfill your basic function in an Afro-Cuban rhythm section. Conversely, all the material presented in the rest of this section on the tumbao will actually <u>impede</u> your ability to create a groove unless the rhythmic patterns already presented are really yours. So please, before you go on, review and practice these first two chapters until they are as natural as walking down the street. The rewards will be great!

CD One
TRACK #15

Guaracha 2-3

47

In this chapter we present other relatively simple rhythmic figures to vary the tumbao groove. These figures are generally used to temporarily vary a more standard tumbao, not as foundation bass lines for a tune. After listening to each track, we suggest that you use the accompaniment on the CD to work on one variation at a time, integrated with a standard tumbao, as Oscar does here. Sample variations are listed at the end of each track's transcription.

Please use these with discretion, especially when your group wants people to be dancing to the music. And remember, a little chili pepper will enhance a sauce, but too much will render it inedible!

CD One
TRACK #16

Son-Montuno 3-2

49

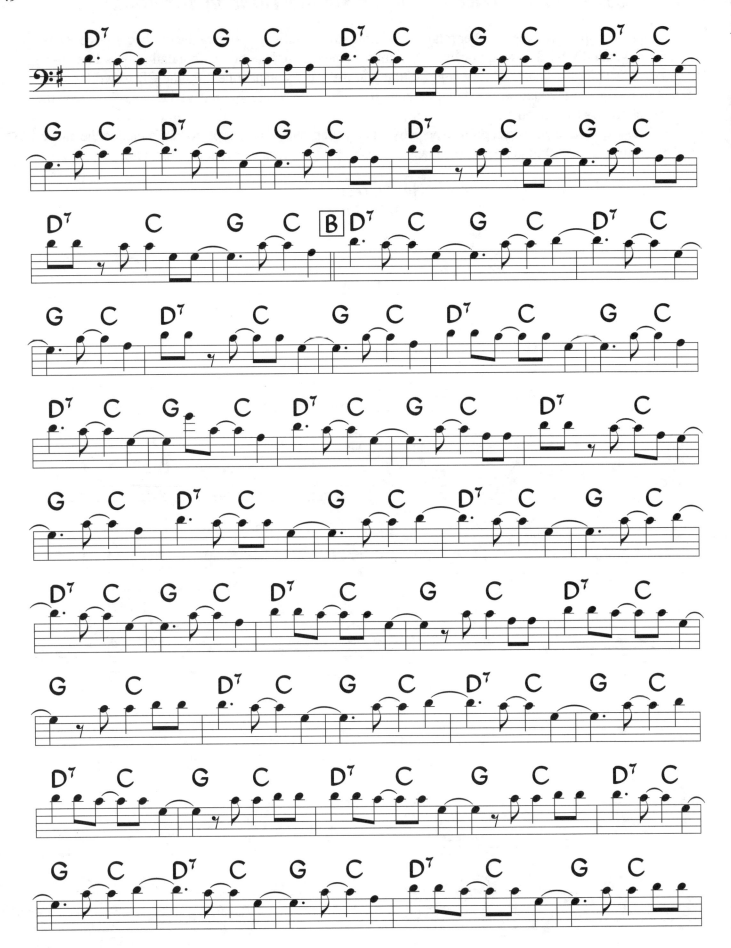

Here are some of the variations that Oscar uses on this track. Try using them one at a time, along with a regular tumbao, when you improvise your own bass line on this exercise.

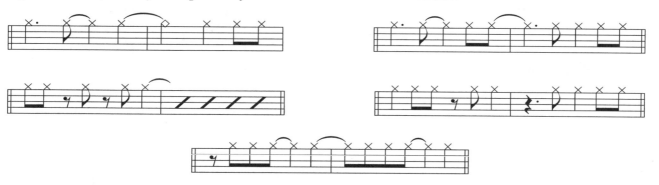

51

Son-Montuno 2-3

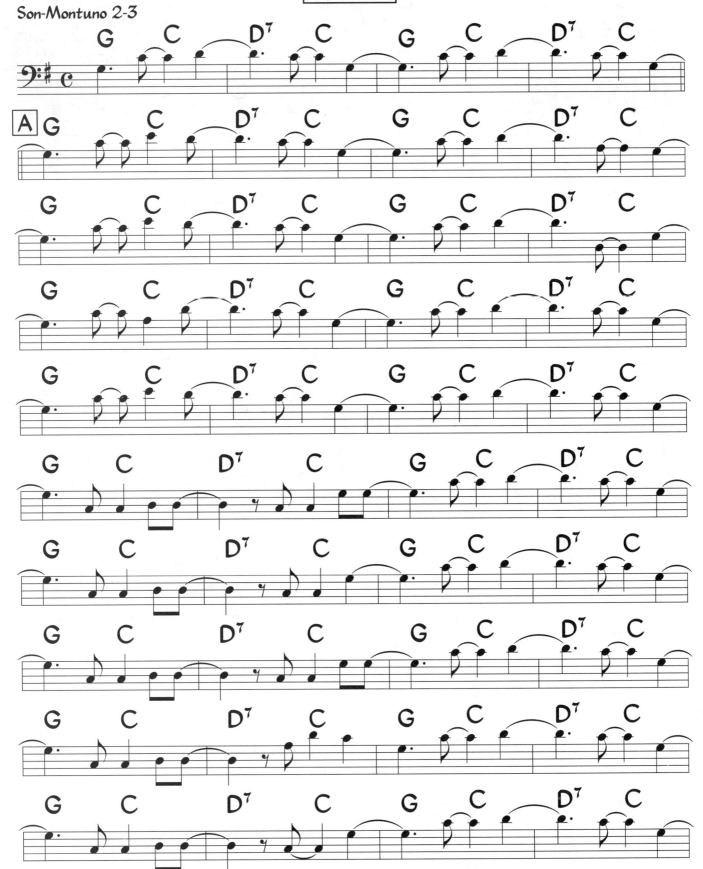

53

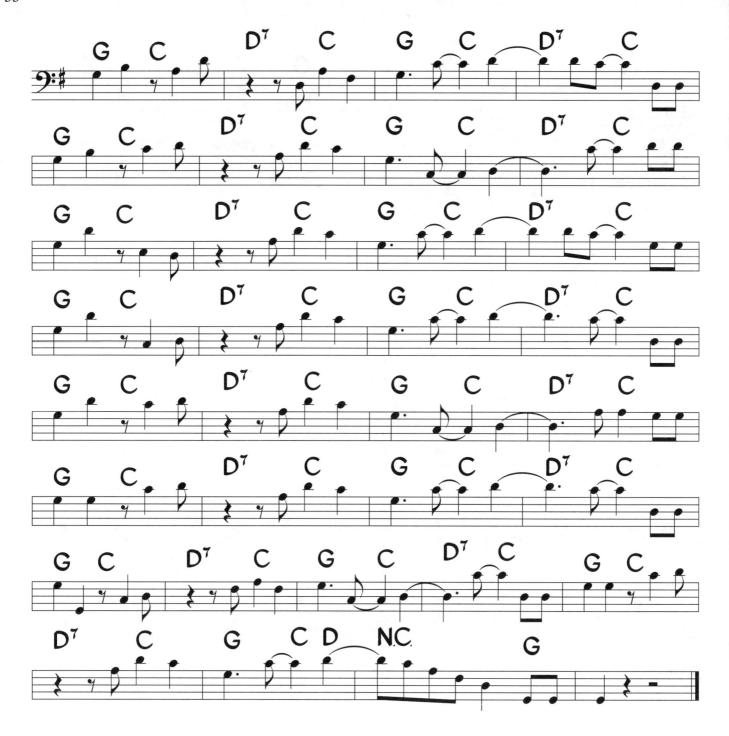

Here are some of the variations that Oscar uses on this track. Try using them one at a time, along with a regular tumbao, when you improvise your own bass line on this exercise.

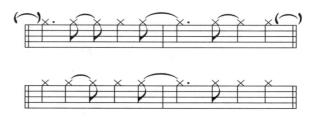

Bomba / Guaracha 3-2

55

Here are some of the variations that Oscar uses on this track. Try using them one at a time, along with a regular tumbao, when you improvise your own bass line on this exercise.

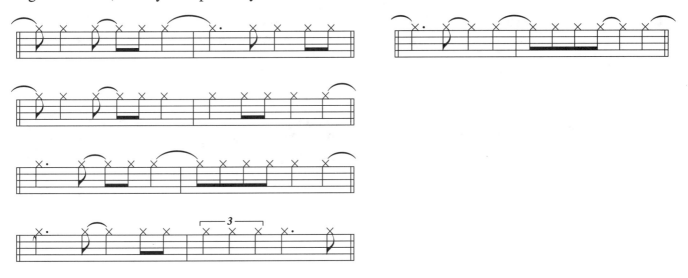

Pilón / Guaracha 2-3

Here are some of the variations that Oscar uses on this track. Try using them one at a time, along with a regular tumbao, when you improvise your own bass line on this exercise.

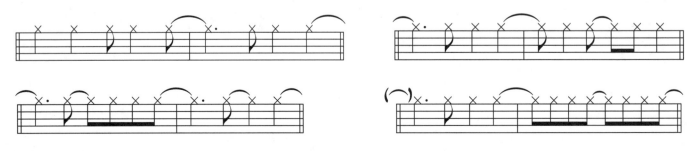

61

Here are some of the variations that Oscar uses on this track. Try using them one at a time, along with a regular tumbao, when you improvise your own bass line on this exercise.

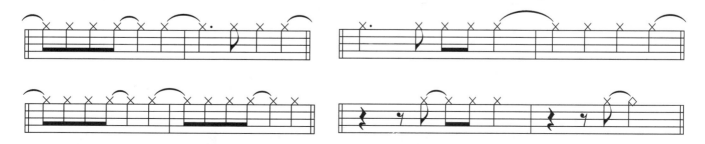

CD One
TRACK #21

Guaracha 2-3

Here are some of the variations that Oscar uses on this track. Try using them one at a time, along with a regular tumbao, when you improvise your own bass line on this exercise.

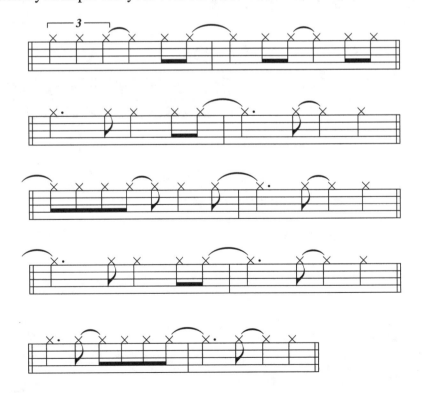

Guaracha 3-2

Here are some of the variations that Oscar uses on this track. Try using them one at a time, along with a regular tumbao, when you improvise your own bass line on this exercise.

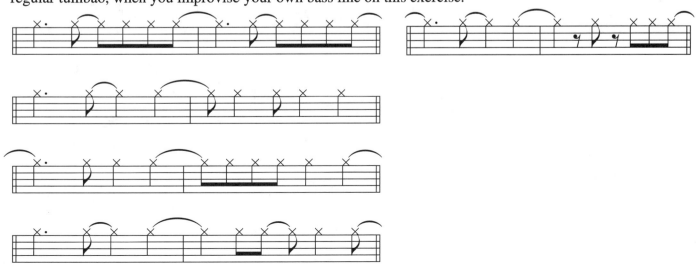

Med-Fast Charanga

70

Here are some of the variations that Oscar uses on this track. Try using them one at a time, along with a regular tumbao, when you improvise your own bass line on this exercise.

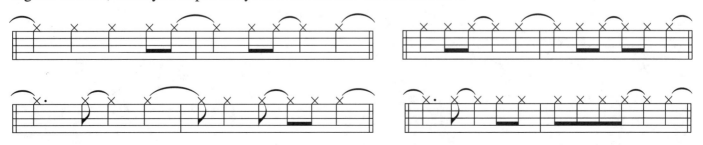

Clave (pronounced klah-vay) is a two measure rhythmic pattern which forms the basis for the parts played by all rhythmic and harmonic instruments (including the voice) in the Afro-Cuban ensemble. The importance of understanding the clave and its variations as the root of rhythm for Afro-Cuban music cannot be overstated.

Here is how the clave pattern looks in 4/4 musical notation:

You should notice that there are 3 beats in the first bar and 2 in the second. This is the (3-2) *Son* clave. *(Son* is pronounced like the word 'zone' with an 's'.) The *Son* is one of the traditional forms of Afro-Cuban music from which contemporary forms have evolved.

This (3-2), sometimes called 'forward', clave pattern may also be played with the measures inverted. That is, 2 beats in the first bar and 3 in the second. This is the (2-3) clave or 'reverse' clave. The terms forward and reverse are not as widely used today, but still may describe the clave's direction.

The clave is an ostinato (repeated) rhythmic pattern which usually does not change from beginning to end in a song. It is traditionally played on the claves, two rounded wooden sticks often made of polished rosewood . The pattern could also be played by a timbale player or a trap drummer on a wooden or plastic block mounted on their instrument.

Although the clave can be considered a finite rhythm "on top of all the other rhythms", it is also essential to feel it as a fundamental "within" the parts each instrument plays. From the bottom (the bass, kick drum and congas) to the top (the voice, flute and trumpet), all are phrasing with and around the clave. It is truly the heartbeat of Afro-Cuban music. Like our own body's heartbeat, for the music to live and breathe the clave must be present and felt, even if not directly heard. In much of Afro-Cuban ensemble playing you will not hear anyone playing the clave directly, yet at the same time all are playing it in their instruments' rhythmic phrasing.

The third variation in the clave is known as the 'rumba' clave. It is similar to 3-2 except the third accent on the three side (bar 1), normally on beat 4, is displaced by one eighth note to the eighth note after 4—the 'and of 4'.

rumba clave

This clave, although primarily used in the folkloric singing, drumming and dancing form known as rumba, has evolved to also be used in contemporary salsa and Latin jazz. It must be noted here that the term 'salsa' literally refers to the condiment or sauce used in cooking and later was applied as slang to identify and commercialize Afro-Cuban music.

The final clave variation we will discuss is the 6/8 clave. It is the same as the 6/8 bell pattern. This clave has interesting notational variations, as it can be seen written in 6/8 time signature, or as 6/4, 12/8 and even 3/4. We've seen them all used by various arrangers.

Although the 6/8 clave pattern is often written in it's own time signature, an important concept to grasp is the ability to hear and play it with a 4/4 pulse, subdivided into two parts. Let's talk for a moment about the concept of 'pulse'.

In general, pulse can be considered as an elongated subdivision of the time signature. For example, in 4/4 the pulse for swing time is on beats 2 and 4. In straight time, as in Afro-Cuban music, the pulse is on 1 and 3, half notes. In each of the above examples, the pulse, although written to reflect the time signature, is felt in exactly the same place. The utilization of this pulse as an adjunct to the time signature helps the music to feel more smooth and keeps track of where the bars start and finish without the necessity of counting or feeling each beat individually. Another way to describe the pulse is a half-time feel. It really makes the music lay better!

In 6/8 as well, the pulse is felt in "2", each one a dotted quarter note. As you can see, two of these underlying pulses are found in each bar, with four pulses for the entire two bar clave pattern.

Again, here is how the 6/8 clave and pulse line up together.

Practice patting your foot in the various time signatures along with the 6/8 clave. There is only a notational difference. The rhythm and the pulse are the same for them all.

6/8 clave may also be considered to be forward or reverse. You see in our examples it is still a two bar pattern (except for 12/8). You may also play starting with the second bar first (reverse). This is somewhat rare but it may happen.

Now that we've looked at clave and it's variations, how does it relate to the bass? The part or line the bass plays is called the 'tumbao' and utilizes the rhythm of the clave pattern in a very direct way. In the *Son* clave you remember there are 5 accented beats, 3 in the first bar and 2 in the second. Two of these accents have their own names. The accent which falls on the 'and of 2' of the three side (first bar) is called 'bombo'. The bass plays this accent. The accent which falls on beat 4 of the three side is called 'ponche' and is also played by the bass.

The standard syncopated tumbao we learned in Chapter One uses these accents and so is sometimes called the 'bombo-ponche' tumbao. To begin the pattern you play on beat one of the first bar. From there on however, you are only playing on the 'and of 2' and '4'—bombo and ponche—and tying the notes over the barlines. At this point you are not playing on beat one at all. To keep your place in the time you must know at all times where the beginning of each bar is. This is where your understanding and utilization of the pulse comes into direct play—one of your pulses is on beat one of every measure! You should also take important notice that the tumbao falls exactly with clave on the three side, but not on the two side, as you can see here.

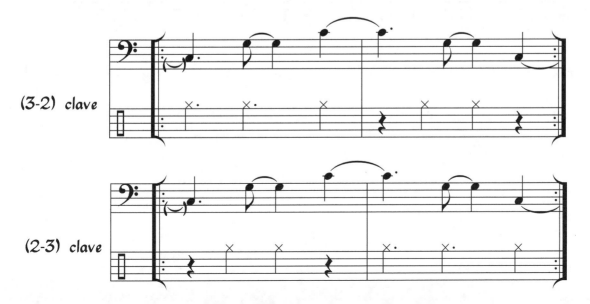

Once again, you start the pattern on beat one, play the 'and of 2' and '4', 'never' again to play on '1', but using your sense of the pulse to keep track of each measure as they fly by. Where is one? You will learn to know it well!

This basic tumbao is the same in both directions of the clave. The parts each of the other instruments plays, i.e. congas, cascara (side of the timbales), compana (hand bell), piano montuno, etc. are two bar phrases which must be played starting on the correct side of the clave. Here, however, we see the bass appearing to be clave 'independent'. We know, however, that all parts are clave related.

Phrasing a more complex tumbao to clave can be tricky and requires clave knowledge and feel. There are no hard and fast rules regarding this issue, but in general the concept is to phrase the tumbao bass line so its major rhythmic accents fall directly in line with clave.

Here are some examples with the clave superimposed in the correct and incorrect direction so you can see and feel the difference.

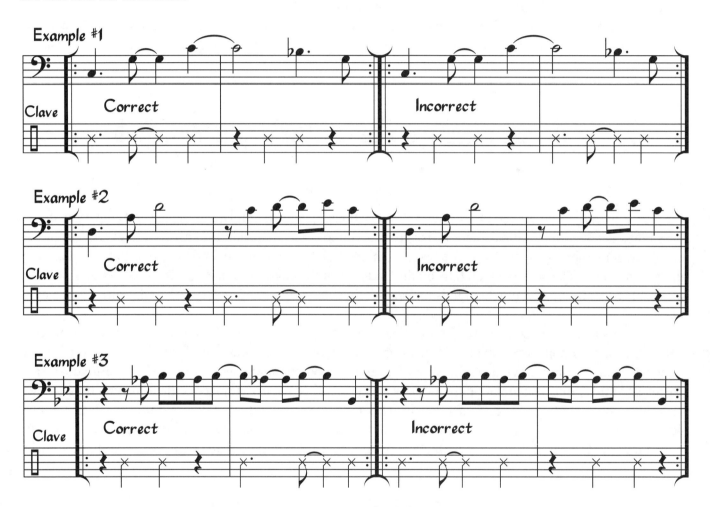

Let's look at some examples in Chapter Three and Five along with their CD tracks to understand their clave.

Taking some sample rhythms played on CD One-Track #16, we have strong rhythmic alignment of beat 1, the 'and of 2' and 4 in measure one, and also beat 3 in measure two. These are all accents of clave. In this example, the chord progression also dictates the clave—a V-IV-I progression is typically 3-2. It feels right, probably because the resolution of the harmony matches the resolution of the rhythm on a strong pulse (beat 3)—the last accent of a 3-2 clave pattern.

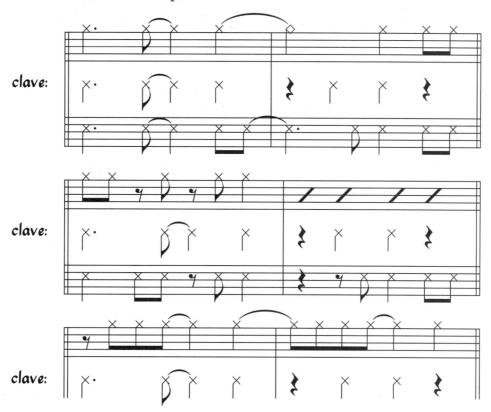

In CD One-Track #17 we see the strong alignments of the 'and of 2' and 4 in bar two. These are also clave accents. Here again the tradition of this chord progression (I-IV-V) makes the clave 2-3, the exact opposite of the previous example. The variations that Oscar plays were constructed with this in mind.

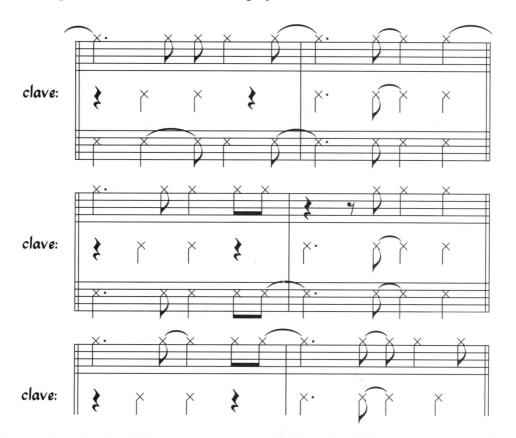

In CD One-Track #18 the bass lines up with clave in beats 1, the 'and of 2', and 4 in bar one, and also beat 2 in measure two. All are accents of clave. Do you see the pattern emerging?

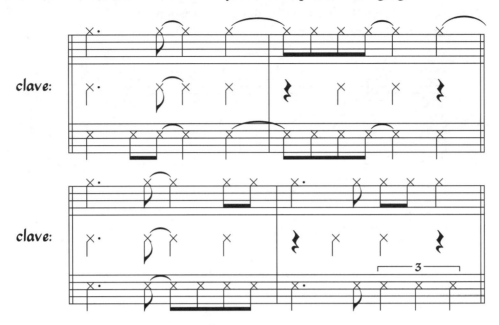

Continue this exploration through the rest of the examples in Chapter Three.

Let's skip now to Chapter Five for advanced variations.

In CD One-Track #24 there are strong clave accents on beats 1 and 'the and of 2' in bar one and also beat 3 in bar two. If you reverse the clave, would it feel as right?

In CD One-Track #25 we have strong clave accents in beats 2 and 3 of bar one and on the 'and of 2' and 4 in bar two. It wouldn't feel right as a 3-2 clave.

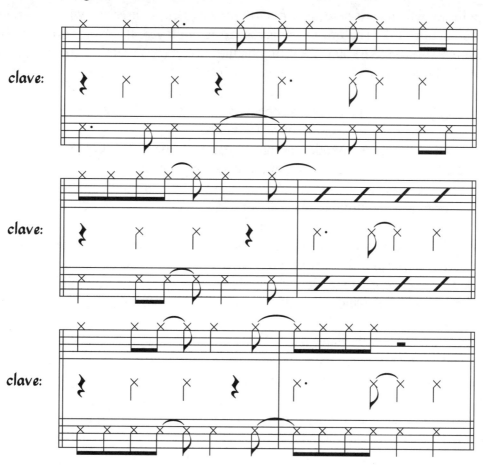

In CD Two, Track #1 the strong clave accents are found in beat 3 of bar one, and also the 'and of 2' and 4 in bar two.

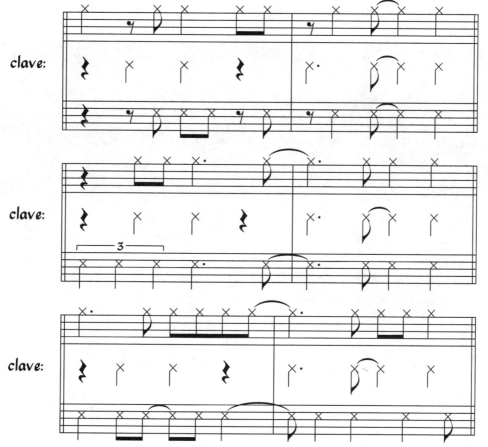

Continue this process with the rest of the examples in Chapter Five and elsewhere in the book.

The last point we will discuss here is the determination of clave direction when it is not known. "(2-3) or (3-2)?" is a question often asked before a song is rehearsed or played. It is a question that should be asked, as all rhythm section parts need to be played starting on the correct bar in relation to clave. If you are looking at an arrangement of a latin jazz or a salsa song, it is assumed that the arranger had clave in mind as he or she created it (we hope.) That clave should be notated at the top of the chart. But very often, especially in the jazz context, you will be looking at fake books or lead sheets with only melodies, chords and perhaps lyrics, and so you will need to figure out what the clave direction should be.

One consideration for clave direction is that of harmonic or chord progression that we touched on earlier in this chapter. There is a good discussion of this and many other aspects of bass and clave in "The True Cuban Bass", by Silvio Vergara and the great Cuban bassist Carlos Del Puerto, published by Sher Music Co. This book is a must for bassists aspiring to learn about Cuban music.

Whether a song is played (3-2) or (2-3) depends primarily on how the melody falls rhythmically in relation to the clave. This process is a subject for trial and error, discussion, and sometimes controversy. First, establish the clave, then sing or play the melody along with it. Then try it with the clave in the other direction. Sometimes the answer is obvious as the main rhythmic accents of the melody fall easily or perfectly with clave in one direction or the other. Other times the answer may be more nebulous as it either fits both ways or seems not to fit easily with either one.

Understanding and feeling the clave in conjunction with your bass tumbaos is quite a learning experience. This process involves both the analytical as well as the artistic sides of the brain. Like anything new that is really worthwhile, it may be difficult at first to understand these concepts, and put them to use. Just keep at it and you will find the pieces slowly falling into place. The key is practice: play along with the CDs in this book, program a drum machine with the rhythms (get a percussionist to help), and when you are ready, start playing with other musicians. Here is where the real joy of this music lives—in the dialogues you create with other musicians who speak the same musical language. With these experiences, you will learn to construct lines using simple to more complex building blocks of rhythmic variations (always with the clave in mind) to create your own great tumbaos.

Dave Belove, author of Chapter 4

CHAPTER FIVE - Advanced Tumbao Variations

Even more than in Chapter 3, the rhythms written at the end of each exercise in this chapter would probably not be played very often in dance-oriented salsa. Rather, they might be used in a more jazz-oriented Latin setting, where the strict tumbao is not so crucial. Use with caution! (On the other hand, they sure are cool!)

As before, feel free to use the play-along tracks for whatever you want after you have gone through what Oscar played on them originally and after you are comfortable with each of the rhythmic variations shown at the end of each transcription.

Here are some of the variations that Oscar uses on this track. Try using them one at a time, along with a regular tumbao, when you improvise your own bass line on this exercise.

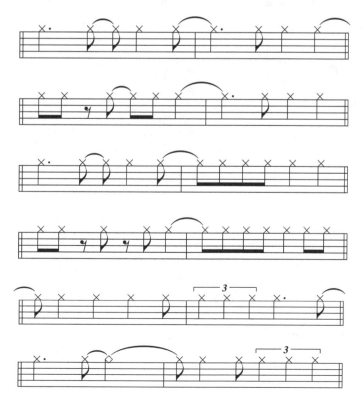

Here are some of the variations that Oscar uses on this track. Try using them one at a time, along with a regular tumbao, when you improvise your own bass line on this exercise.

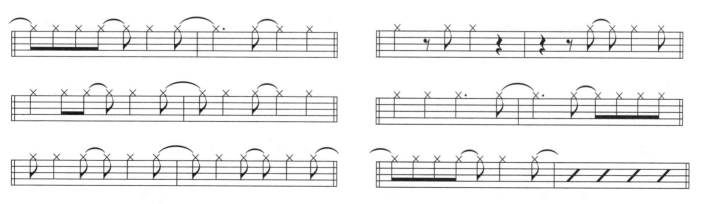

Paquito D'Rivera and Oscar Stagnaro

89

Here are some of the variations that Oscar uses on this track. Try using them one at a time, along with a regular tumbao, when you improvise your own bass line on this exercise.

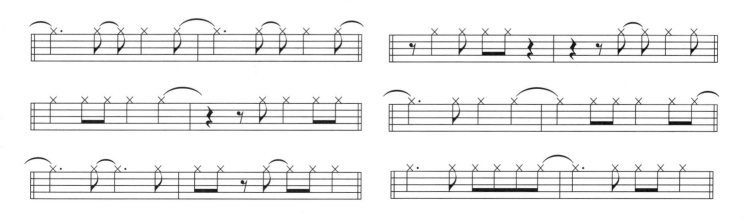

Guaracha 3-2

92

Here are some of the variations that Oscar uses on this track. Try using them one at a time, along with a regular tumbao, when you improvise your own bass line on this exercise.

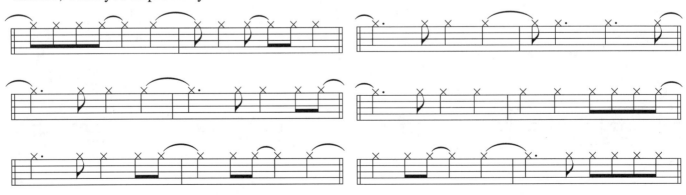

Guaracha 2-3
(perc. break)

Here are some of the variations that Oscar uses on this track. Try using them one at a time, along with a regular tumbao, when you improvise your own bass line on this exercise.

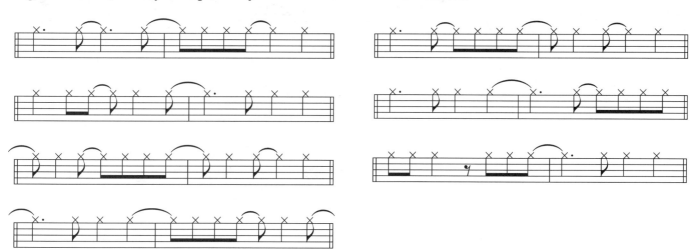

Guaracha 2-3

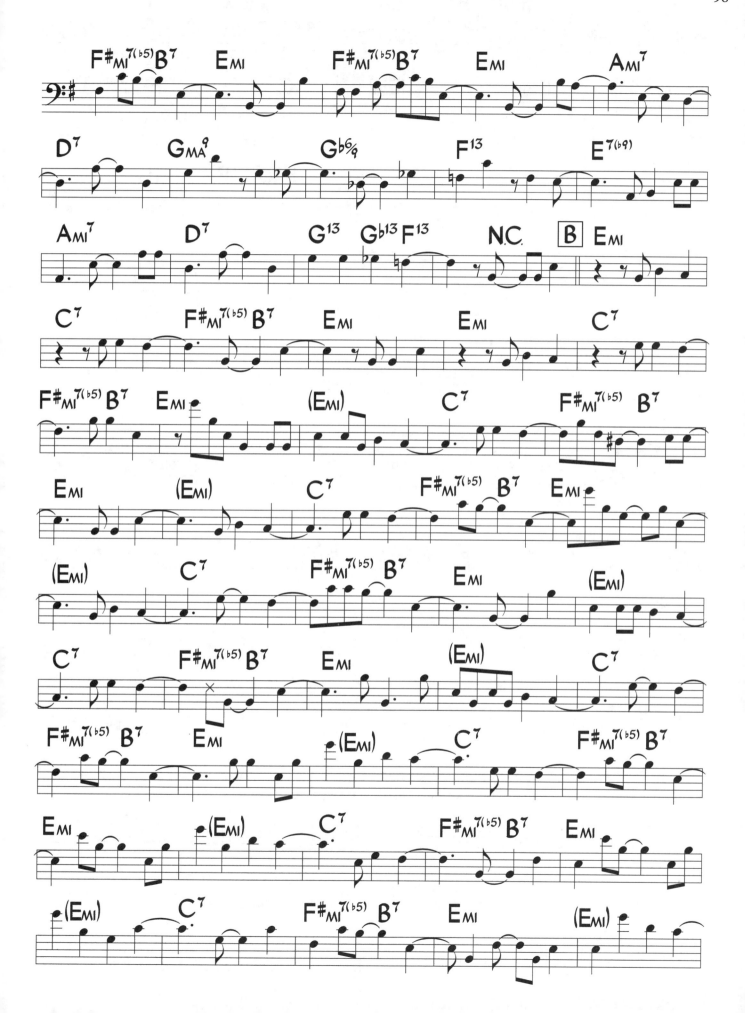

99

Here are some of the variations that Oscar uses on this track. Try using them one at a time, along with a regular tumbao, when you improvise your own bass line on this exercise.

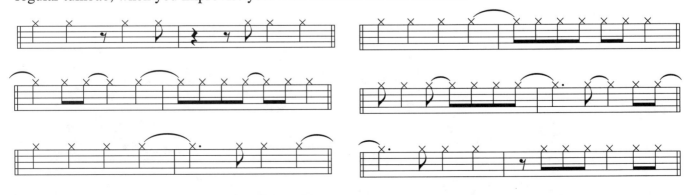

Guaracha 3-2

101

Here are some of the variations that Oscar uses on this track. Try using them one at a time, along with a regular tumbao, when you improvise your own bass line on this exercise.

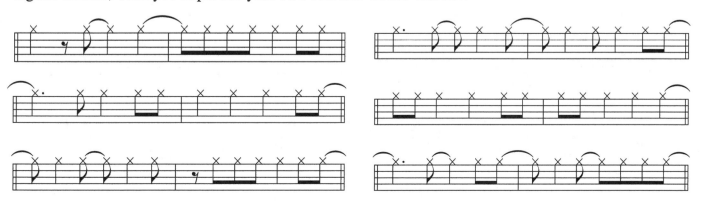

103

Following are some beautiful but relatively complex bass lines for you to study and add to your repertoire (with due caution for the groove, of course!). There is no CD track for these phrases but try playing the rhythms with any CD track you want.

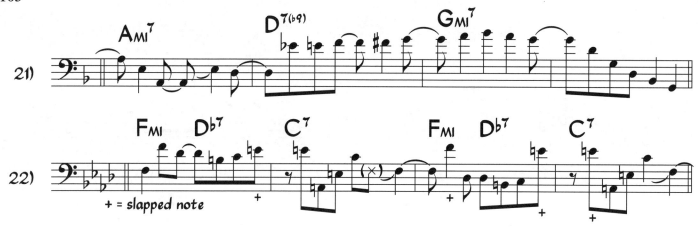

21)

22)

+ = slapped note

The following are bass fills, not tumbao variations

SECTION TWO - OTHER AFRO-CUBAN STYLES

CHAPTER SIX - Cha-Cha-Chá and its Variations

The original cha-cha-chá bass rhythms are as follows:

When you play along with the following track, mix these variations together as your ear dictates. There is no clave direction in a cha-cha-chá.

On this next track, the bass will go through the variations shown below, each one integrated into a more standard cha-cha-chá groove. As before, after you have listened to Oscar play through the exercise, go back and play each variation through the entire track until it is firmly embedded in your subconscious. Otherwise, the odds are that you won't retain this information when you need it - on the gig!

The rhythm below is widely used in cha-cha-chás, as well as bossa nova and other styles of music. It is usually used in combination with other cha-cha-chá rhythms instead of by itself.

These rhythms are a more modern version of the cha-cha-chá, where the "and of 2" is tied to beat 3.

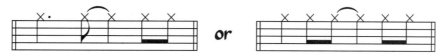

This is the same as variation #2, but the "and of 4" is tied to beat 1 of the next bar. Typically this is played as a two bar figure with no tie between bars 2 and 3.

Adding extra eighth notes leading up to the "and of 2" and beat 4 or the "and of 4" creates a busier, jazz-like version of the cha-cha-chá, heard in a lot of contemporary Latin music. (The rhythm written here is only one possibility among many.)

As with the tumbao, you can and should make up and practice more four bar phrases for yourself, using the material given.

111

Here is an exercise using the variations we have looked at so far and some new ones as well.

113   Here is Oscar playing on the chord changes to Peruchin's arrangement of "Dejala Que Siga Andando" by Mendez & Bolaños. Again, it will be worth your while to take the rhythm of each four bar phrase of this transcription and play it through the entire track until it is yours.

114

115

Here are a few more miscellaneous cha-cha-chá bass lines that you should look at and add to your list of possibilities. (There is no CD track for these phrases.)

(old style cha-cha-chá)

CHAPTER SEVEN - *Afro Lines in 6*

The African influence in Afro-Cuban music is most strongly felt in those pieces that are played in 6/8 (sometimes written as 3/4 or 12/8). The basic pulse is usually two dotted quarter notes per bar subdivided into two groups of three eighth notes each, as follows:

The rhythmic complexity appears when you play three notes against this basic two pulse, as follows:

As you can see, these triplets (three against a two pulse) are written here as quarter notes and can easily become the dominant pulse that you feel, but be sure you can also feel them as a polyrhythm against the basic two beats per bar. It is the rhythmic tension of two against three that gives the Afro 6/8 groove its intensity. The following exercises are designed to show you how this all works. As before, integrating the rhythms written at the end of the transcriptions into your own playing is what will help you the most. So make sure you work on each of them, one at a time.

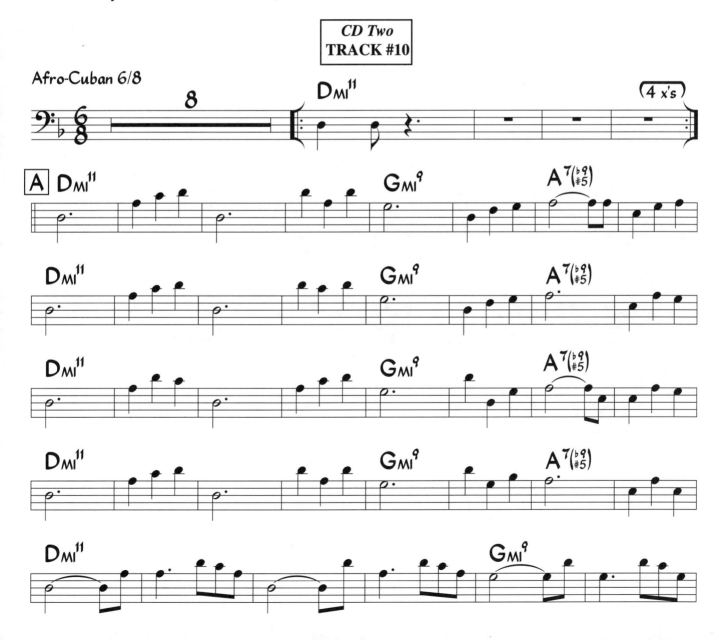

117

Here are some two bar 6/8 figures for you to practice along with this track.

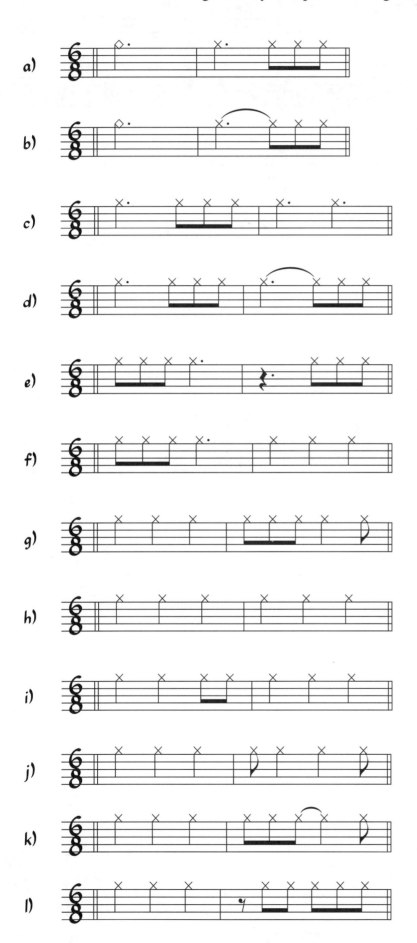

Ray Barretto and Oscar Stagnaro

Next, we have some 6/8 figures with more advanced syncopations in them. Be sure you can feel the two pulses in each bar, even when three quarter notes per bar are used.

124

125

Here are some variations to try when playing along with the previous track.

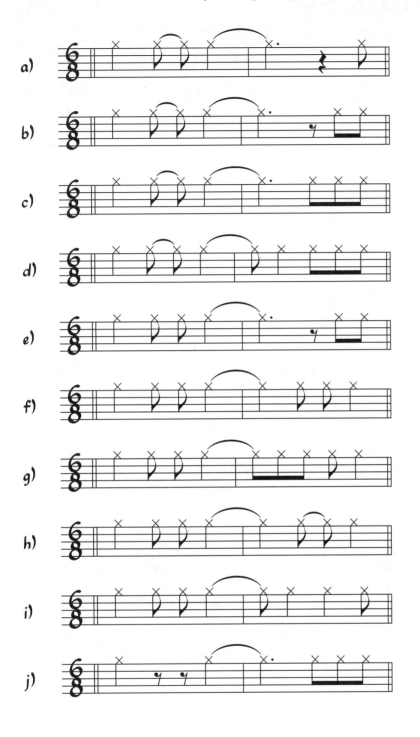

On this track we will go from a sixteen bar 4/4 guaracha to a sixteen bar 6/8 phrase. Notice that the two basic pulses per bar stay the same throughout this time change, i.e., original half note = new dotted quarter note.

Guaracha 3-2 / 6/8

CD Two
TRACK #12

127

CHAPTER EIGHT - Contemporary Cuban-Style Bass Lines

Starting in the 1970s, first in Cuba and then in the rest of the Latin music world, the strict bass tumbao gradually has given way to newer types of bass lines, at least among the younger, "cutting edge" dance bands. The most widespread of these forms of Cuban music is the Songo. This next track will give you a sample of this groove, originated by bassist Juan Formell, leader of the Cuban band Los Van Van.

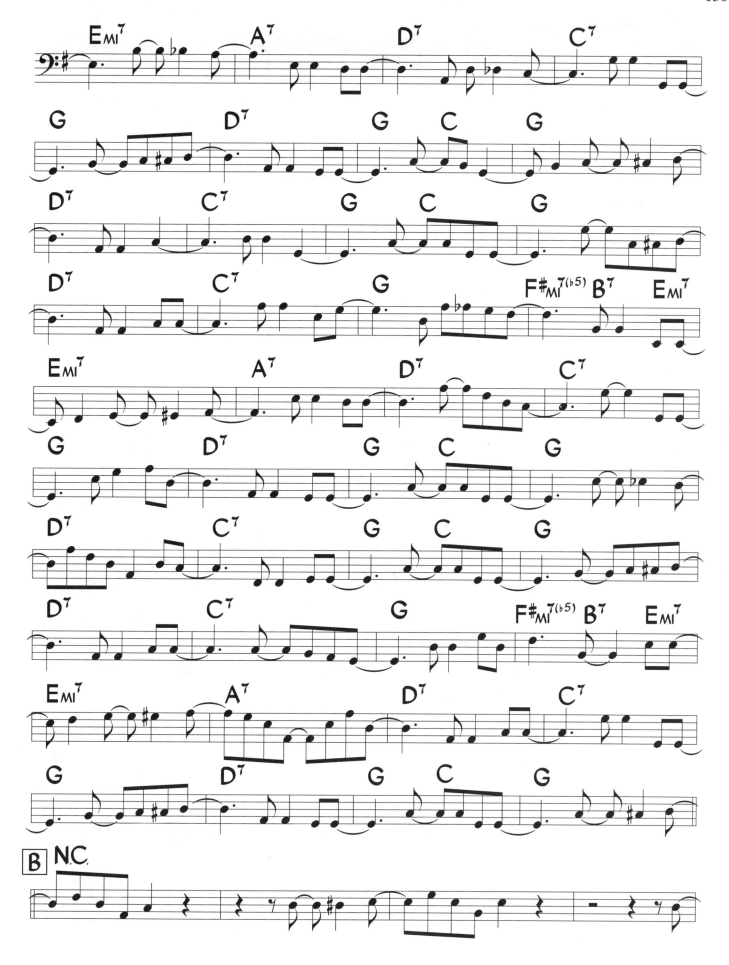

Here are some recorded Songo-style bass lines for you to study, along with short descriptions of each. There is no CD track for these short examples but try playing the rhythmic approach of one of them at a time along with a CD track from this chapter.

a) Notice the use of arpeggios here as well as beat 4 and

La Resolucion (2-3)

Que es lo que tiene (2-3)

Note the use of the major 7th here as well as the '4 and' figure tied to the next bar.

The rhythm of bars 1 and 3 here are often played by Juan Formel.

c) Tumbao-like line but using more space gives it a different swing. Note the use of the F on the G7 chord.

El Buena Gente (2-3)

d) Notice here that the 'and of 4' is tied over from the first bar of this two bar pattern, but not on the second bar.

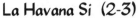

e) Note the use of arpeggios here, the tied over note on the 'and of 4' and the timbales rhythm in bars 3, 4 and 6.

f) This is like a montuno line that defines the harmony by itself, using various versions of 7th chords.

g) This excerpt uses quarter notes typical of the Timba groove, mixed with eighth notes typical of the Songo and the rhythm of the Bomba in bar 2.

This second excerpt from the same tune uses a busier line with eighth note anticipations.

135

h) Notice that this line uses the 3rd of the chord instead of the root in the second bar.

Esto te pone la cabeza mala (2-3)

Here is a second variation of this idea, using a rhythm in bars 3 and 4 that is almost like a Soca feel.

i) A combination of a Cachao-like descarga rhythm with a Bomba in bar 2 and a Timba feel in bar 3.

Mandalo y ven (2-3)

j) Note the arpeggio in bar 1 and the use of the fifth of the chord to start bar 3.

Que le den candela (3-2)

Here are some other "post-tumbao" Cuban-style bass lines for you to look over.

Sal Cuevas / Agua a la Candela / Sonora Ponceña (2-3)

Sal Cuevas / Soy Dichoso / Ray Barreto (2-3)

Feliciano Arango / Dime lo que tu sabes / Isaac Delgado (3-2)

Feliciano Arango / Dime lo que tu sabes / Isaac Delgado (3-2)

Feliciano Arango / Santa Palabra / NG la Banda (2-3)

Oscar Hernandez / Dile que vuelva / Afrocuba (2-3)

Para Ti / Machito

El Divorcio / Arsenio Rodriguez (2-3)

Reunion / Paquito D'Rivera

Here is another example of Oscar playing in a contemporary Latin dance style, this time featuring his mastery of the slap bass technique.

141

Here is one final example of the Songo style. Notice the rhythmic variations Oscar uses and try to incorporate some of them into your own playing when you go through and play along with this track yourself.

CD Two
TRACK #15

Songo 3-2

142

SECTION THREE - BRAZILIAN BASS LINES

CHAPTER NINE - Samba Bass Lines

The most common samba bass rhythm is shown below. Typically the root is played on beat 1 and the fifth (below the root, if possible) is played on beat 3.

Here is a transcription of Oscar's playing this basic samba groove on the changes to "Rio" by Roberto Menescal & Ronaldo Boscoli. Notice how he articulates each note. Since the note choices and rhythms are pretty simple here, it is the feeling and clarity of each note that makes this groove work.

CD Two
TRACK #16

147

Here is Oscar playing a samba and creating rhythmic interest by varying the basic samba figure somewhat. Try analyzing how he does that on this track and then take one variation at a time through the
changes of this happy little tune.

CD Two
TRACK #17

(Freely)

149 The most common variation of the samba bass groove is to accent beat 3 of each bar. Here are a couple of ways to articulate this idea, which is designed to simulate the sound of the big bass drum, the *surdo*, in a street samba ensemble. On this track Oscar demonstrates how this is done (as well as how to keep a samba rhythmically interesting without sacrificing the groove) on the chords of Gonzaguinha's beautiful tune "E'"

More advanced samba variations

The following tracks include some more advanced variations on the samba groove, the rhythms of which are listed separately at the end of each exercise. These variations are most commonly used as brief contrasts to a more basic samba pattern or perhaps as the basic rhythm for a particular section of a tune, returning then to a more traditional samba bass part. As with the advanced tumbao bass lines, these variations can do more harm than good if not used with discretion.

Here are some rhythmic variations you should try, one at a time, when you play along with the previous track.

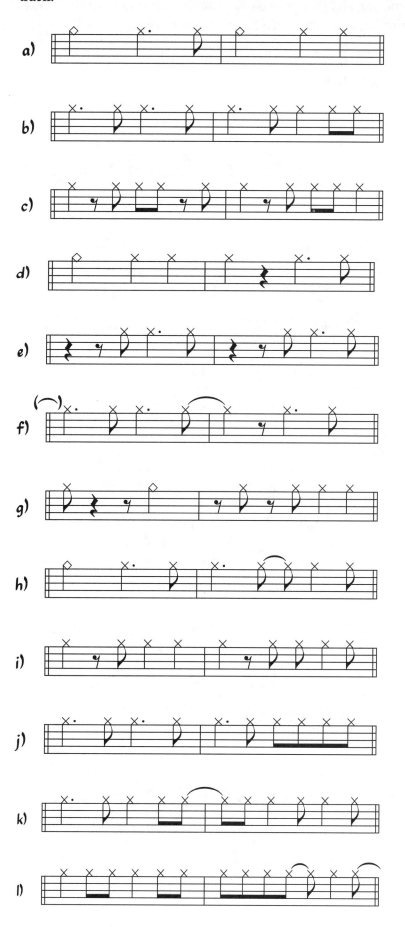

157   Here is a transcription of Oscar playing through the changes of "Samba De Orpheus", using some more adventurous rhythms to spice up the samba groove. If you can't play the transcription up to tempo (quite a feat!), just go through it at whatever tempo you can and then play along with the CD using one rhythm at a time from those listed at the end of the transcription, in addition to a basic samba groove.

158

159

Here are some rhythmic variations you should try, one at a time, when you play along with the previous track.

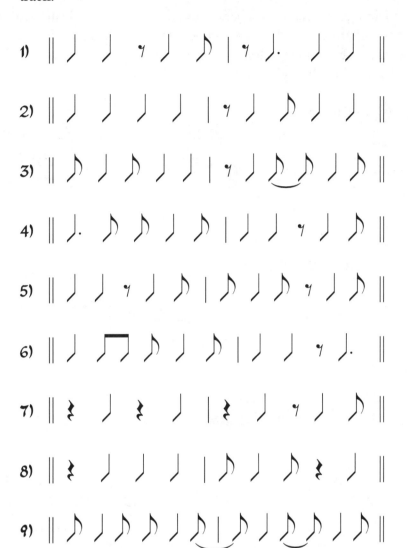

CHAPTER TEN - Partido Alto, Baião and other Brazilian Styles

Forward Partido Alto

Partido Alto is a variation of samba and, in fact, regular samba bass lines are often used while the rest of the rhythm section is playing a Partido Alto. Alternatively, the bass can double the Partido Alto hits as Oscar does on the following track. After listening and playing along with the whole track, go back and isolate particular four bar phrases and play one at a time through this blues form.

Here are the basic variations of the forward Partido Alto rhythm.

162

Carneval in Rio

Photo by Robert Feinberg

Reverse Partido Alto

This is the same rhythm as the forward version but starting on bar 2, instead of bar 1. It is actually much more common than the forward version. The main variations are listed at the end of this transcription. And again, you should practice each of them separately along with the CD track.

Here are some of the variations that Oscar uses on this track. Try using them, one at a time, when you improvise your own bass line on this exercise.

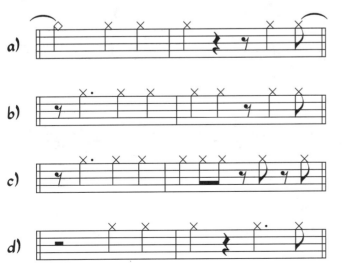

Baião

Here is the basic bass rhythm for the Brazilian style known as the baião.

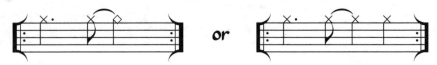

This track features Oscar playing this rhythm on a C blues form.

**CD Two
TRACK #23**

172

173

Here Oscar plays some great variations of the baião bass part on the changes of Milton Nascimento's lovely tune, "Vera Cruz".

CD Three
TRACK #1

174

Here are some of the variations that Oscar uses on this track. Try using them, one at a time, when you improvise your own bass line on this exercise.

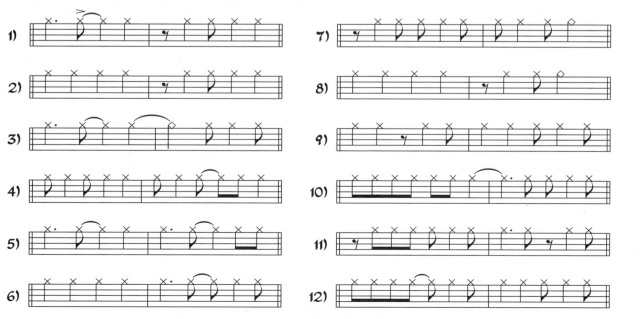

Choro/Chorinho

Here is an example of the choro or chorinho, a style of music developed in the northeastern part of Brazil. It is written in 2/4, as most Brazilian music is notated in Brazil itself. Here Oscar plays on the tune, "Lamentos", written by Pixinguinha.

179

181

Afoxé

Another Brasilian style gaining popularity in the rest of the world is the afoxe. Here Oscar plays in this style on Ivan Lins' tune, "Madelena". Notice the use of the "3, 4" in the afoxé sections.

Oscar Stagnaro

Photo by Ken Franckling

To complete the Brazilian section of the book, here is a piece (based on "rhythm changes"), which mixes a samba with the baião groove, masterfully played by Oscar Stagnaro.

187

SECTION FOUR -
CARIBBEAN & SOUTH AMERICAN STYLES

CHAPTER ELEVEN - *Merengue, Reggae and Other Caribbean Styles*

While the primary purpose of this book is to help you master the bass' role in Afro-Cuban and Brazilian music, we thought that some of the other main Caribbean and South American styles of music should be represented as well. We make no claim to have exhausted the subtleties of these kinds of music here—just some representative examples of each style to get you familiar with the basics.

First is an example of the calypso. Since this is first and foremost music for dancing, notice how Oscar keeps any rhythmic variations from getting in the way of the groove.

190

191

Next is an example of a soca groove, a more contemporary version of calypso.

CD Three
TRACK #6

Here we have an example of how to play a reggae bass part, a style that has a lot of room for bass creativity while still keeping a room full of people dancing. This track is based on Bob Marley's reggae classic, "Could You Be Loved?".

CD Three
TRACK #7

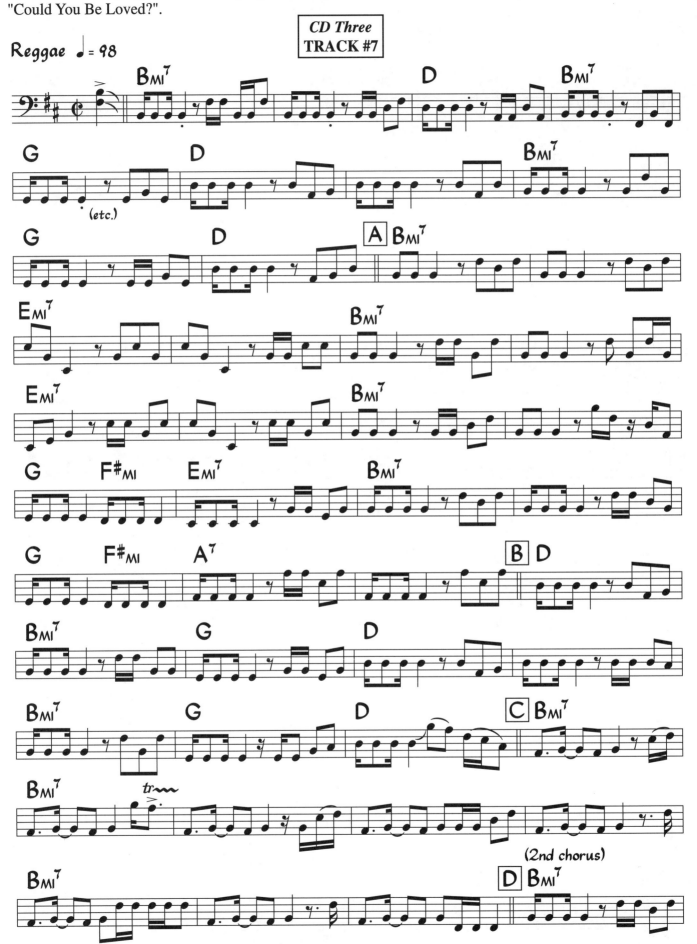

Here are some more typical reggae bass lines, suggested by the multi-talented Attila Nagy. Sample keyboard and drum parts are shown too, so you can see when each kind of line would be appropriate. Reggae is primarily an improvised music—it's about feel. The bass tone should be fat and round and dominant in the mix. Reggae bass lines define the rhythm of a particular tune and are melodic, syncopated ostinato patterns. (Drum hits with a * under them are played on the snare, all others on the kick drum.) There is no CD track here.

#1 One Drop – With the "One Drop" beat (kick drum on the third beat), the first note of the measure for the bass is on the third beat, with the bass drum, implying a hesitation by leaving out the first beat in the measure.

#2 One Drop variation – Another approach for a bass pattern over the "One Drop" beat.

#3 Dub - Dub is a style originating from studio recordings where the engineer would cut out sections of instrumental parts, creating space. In live performance, dub is executed by dropping notes out of the bass pattern or resting for several measures and then coming back with just bass and drums.

#4 Two Four - "Two Four" is like a slow rock ballad. In this example the bass and bass drum play together on the down beat while the snare plays a back beat. The drum beat is akin to the traditional Nyabingi heart beat rhythm.

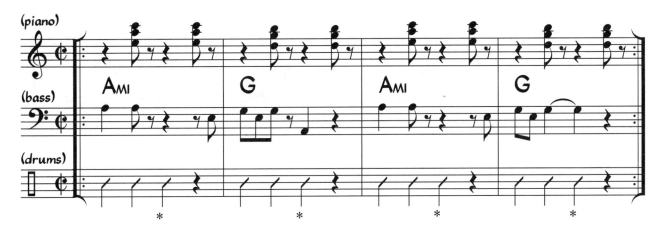

#5 Mix Down - This universal pattern can be recognized as a half clave. In reggae it is used as breaks and under "dance hall" style reggae toasting (rap). Usually all the instruments hit at the same time with bass and drums.

#6 Four On Floor - Four quarter note beats on the kick drum with the bass playing on down beats with syncopated grace notes.

#7 Ska - Ska is a predecessor of Reggae and has remained popular over the years. It's like Reggae played in double time. On many early Ska recordings the bass plays a walking quarter note pattern. Other times the pattern is more syncopated, playing off the vocals or horn parts. The same pattern as #6 works with the Ska beat as well.

For reference on reggae bass, listen to Jamaican originators of the style, like Familyman Barret of the Wailers, Robbie Shakespear, or Fully Fulwood.

Juan Formell of Los Van Van

199

Here is an example of one of the most popular dance styles in the world, the merengue, from the Dominican Republic. Notice Oscar's use of rhythmic displacement to create interest while still holding up the bottom. (But be cautious about using them if you are playing for dancers.)

CHAPTER TWELVE - *South American Styles*

In this chapter we present some very interesting music from various countries of South America. These styles are not as well known in the rest of the world as the ones we have studied earlier, but after going through them, we're sure you'll be glad you did.

For this version of the merengue, originally from Caracas, Venezuela, some people believe that it is in 5/8 with a laid back eighth note at the end of the bar and others that it is a short 6/8. The basic bass pattern is a dotted quarter note and a quarter note in the same bar, but sometimes the bass anticipates the next bar, giving it a tumbao-like feel. The modern instrumentation for this style of music is usually mandolin, cuatro, flute and acoustic guitar.

207

Here is a faster version of the same style.

CD Three
TRACK #10

209

Here is a list of groups and bass players from South America that you should listen to if you want to explore these styles further.

Country	Group or recording artist	Bassist
Venezuela	Gurrufio Ensemble	David Pena
	Aldemaro Romero	Mike Vertiz
	Maroa	Alejandro Rodriguez
	Cecilia Todd	Roberto Cox
	El Guaco	Carlos Pucci
	Aquiles Baez	Alexis Escalona
	El Cuarteto	Telesforo Naranjo
	Un solo Pueblo	Florentino Perales
		Lorenzo Barrientos
	Omar Acosta	Jesus Gonzales
	Onkora	Roberto Koch
	Pabellon sin Baranda	
	Simon Diaz	
	Marco Granados	
Argentina	Raul Carnota	Juancito Farias Gomez
	Cesar Franov	Cesar Franov
	Mercedes Sosa	Carlos Genoni
	Lucho Hoyos	Javier Nunez
		Willy Gonzales
Peru	Susana Baca	David Pinto
	Zambo Cavero y Oscar Aviles	Juan Rebaza
		Walter Fuentes
	Eva Ayllon	Felipe Pomarada
	Nicomedes Santa Cruz	Carlos Hayre
	Andres Soto	Pepe Hernandez

211

Next is a sample of another Venezuelan style, the Joropo. This is the most typical of the Venezuelan rhythms and it has alot of variations—Tuyero, Llanero, Guayanes and Oriental. The Joropo is in 3/4 and originally was played by the harp, bandola, cuatro, maracas and singers. The bass usually plays on beats 1 and 3. Sometimes the Joropo changes the feel to 6/8 and the bass will then play on what was beats 2 and 3, (still counting in 3/4.)

CD Three
TRACK #11

213

214

215

Also from Venezuela, here is an example of the Pajarillo. A form of Joropa, the Pajarillo is a fast 3/4, mainly a I-IV-V progression in a minor key that modulates to major at the bridge. It is a showcase for the virtuosity of the harp and cuatro.

216

217

The last Venezuelan piece in the book is called a Gaita, originally from Maracaibo, located on the west coast of Venezuela. It is a festive rhythm that is played mostly during Christmas. It may have been influenced by or have influenced the Tumba from Curaçao. A very typical instrument called the furruco plays the bass part. The rest of the ensemble is usually the charrasaca, güiro, maracas, cuatro and tambor de gaita.

CD Three
TRACK #13

221

From the province of Salta in the northern part of Argentina, close to Bolivia, comes the style known as Zamba. The Zamba is a slow and romantic type of music in 6/8 (or 3/4) where the bass is primarily responsible for playing on beat 1 of each bar.

CD Three
TRACK #14

223

From the province of Argentina known as Santiago del Estero comes the kind of music known as the Chacarera. It is played in a medium or fast tempo in 6/8 and the bass plays the bottom part of the rhythm played by the Bombo.

225

From Peru, Oscar Stagnaro's home country, comes a type of music called the Lando. Originally from Chincha, it is an old art form that re-appeared in the 1960s after the recording of El Toro Mata. It is very similar to Tondero and Resbalosa and is a sensual and romantic dance in 6/8. It is performed by a lead singer with a call and response format. It is usually played by an ensemble consisting of singers, acoustic guitars, bass, cajon, cajita and quijada.

226

227

Also from Peru comes our final South American piece, a happy groove called Festejo. This is an Afro-Peruvian rhythm originally from the Central Coast of Peru which has a large black population from the days of colonization. It is in 12/8 and uses a percussion instrument called the cajon. It is usually played by an ensemble consisting of vocals, guitar, cajon, quidada (donkey jaw), cajita and bass. Rescued from obscurity by Porfirio Vasquez at the end of the 1940s, the Festejo narrates the events of daily life.

229

SECTION FIVE - LATIN JAZZ BASS LINES

CHAPTER THIRTEEN - Latin Jazz Bass Lines

Latin music has influenced jazz greatly through the years and jazz players have developed their own way of playing or insinuating Latin rhythms in a jazz context. These are usually less strict and repetitive than traditional Latin bass lines. Jaco Pastorius, Eddie Gomez, Stanley Clarke and Ron Carter, to name but a few, have played some amazing music in this style.

What follows are some of the more memorable bass lines in the Latin jazz style, all in D minor. Read through them all first, then take one at a time (and variations on it) through any CD track you want, making adjustments for the type of chords involved, of course. There is no CD track for these lines.

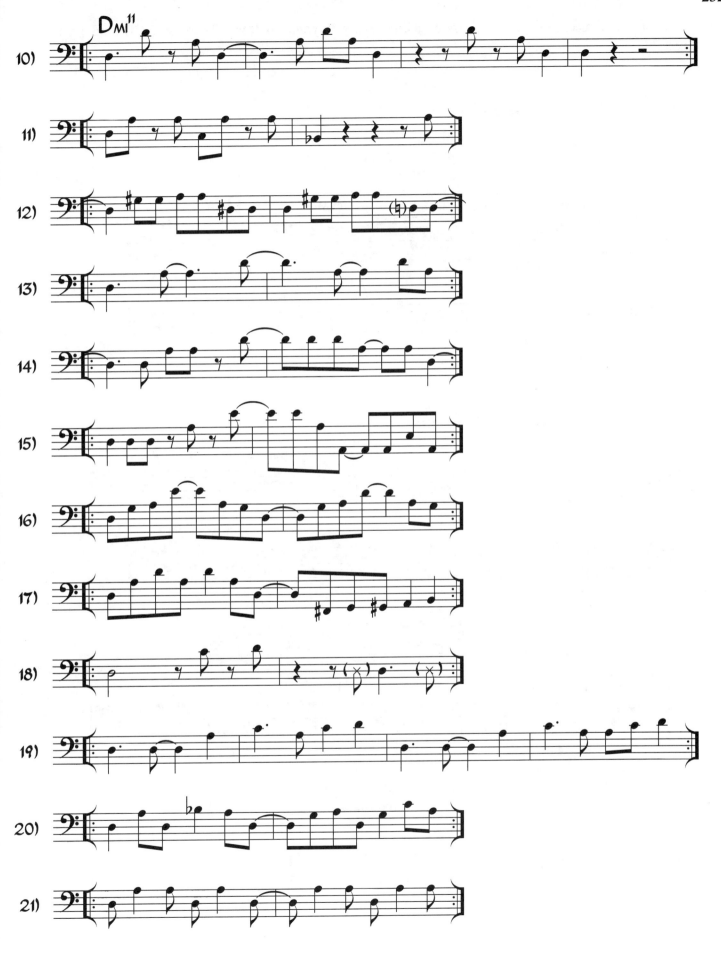

233

Here are some miscellaneous Latin jazz bass lines to add to your repertoire. There is no CD track for these lines.

Carlos Del Puerto

235   To give you a state-of-the-art Latin jazz bass line to study, here Oscar is featured on the changes of Horace Silver's beautiful tune, "Nica's Dream". Notice how many of the rhythms we have studied earlier appear here. Even if you can't read Oscar's line up to tempo, use the track to make up your own bass lines in this style.

236

238

APPENDIX I - RECORDED BASS LINES

PEDRO PEREZ' bass line on "LA RUMBA ESTA BUENA" from Descarga Boricua's CD "Esta Si Va!"

243

245

ANDY GONZALEZ' bass line on "LITTLE SUNFLOWER" from Manny Oquendo & Libre's CD "Ritmo, Sonido y Estilo"

246

249

OSCAR STAGNARO'S bass line on "SIN SABER PORQUE" from Victor Mendoza's CD, "This Is Why"

251

(Vibes solo continued)

253

(Sax solo continued)

(Sax solo continued)

(Piano solo)

ANDY GONZALEZ' bass line on "RAINSVILLE" from Don Grolnick's CD "Medianoche"
(bass line on solos only, not melody)

(Head)

ANDY GONZALEZ' bass line on "WATER BABIES" from Don Grolnick's CD, "Medianoche"

259

(Vibes solo) (1 chorus)

261

APPENDIX II - Oscar Stagnaro Discography

United Nations Orchestra	"Live at MCG In Pittsburg"
	"A Night In Englewood" (Messidor Records) with Slide Hampton
Paquito D'Rivera	"100 Years Of Latin Love Songs" (Heads Up Records)
	"Live At The Blue Note" (Half Note Records)
	"The Music Of Paquito D'Rivera" (Jamey Aebersold Play-Along, #75)
Dave Valentin	"Musical Portraits" (GRP Records)
Los Hijos del Sol	"Los Hijos del Sol" (Sono Sur Records) with Wayne Shorter and Ernie Watts
Charlie Sepulveda	"Algo Nuestro" (Antilles Records) with David Sanchez
The Caribbean Jazz Project	"Island Stories" (Heads Up Records)
	"The Caribbean Jazz Project" (Heads Up Records)
Dan Moretti	"Brasilia" (Brownstone Records)
	"Saxual" (Brownstone Records)
Richie Zellon	"Cafe Con Leche" (Songosaurus Records)
	"The Nazca Lines" (Songosaurus Records) with George Garzone
	"Metal Caribe" (Songosaurus Records) with Dave Liebman
Victor Mendoza	"If Only You Knew" (RAM Records) with Danilo Perez
	"This Is Why" (RAM Records)
Juan Pablo Torres	"Trombone Man" (RMM-Sony Records)
Andy Narell	"Fire In The Engine Room" (Heads Up Records)
Aquiles Baez	"Taratara"
Wayne Naus	"Heart And Fire"
Patricia Saravia	"Rhythm Of The Saints" (Songosaurus Records)
Oscar Feldman	"The Angel" (Songosaurus Records) with Gato Barbieri & Cluadio Roditi
Oscar Stagnaro	"Mariella's Dream" (Songosaurus Records)

SHER MUSIC Co. – The finest in Jazz & Latin Publications

THE NEW REAL BOOK SERIES

The Standards Real Book (C, Bb or Eb)

A Beautiful Friendship
A Time For Love
Ain't No Sunshine
Alice In Wonderland
All Of You
Alone Together
At Last
Baltimore Oriole
Bess, You Is My Woman
Bluesette
But Not For Me
Close Enough For Love
Crazy He Calls Me
Dancing In The Dark

Days Of Wine And Roses
Dreamsville
Easy To Love
Embraceable You
Falling In Love With Love
From This Moment On
Give Me The Simple Life
Have You Met Miss Jones?
Hey There
I Can't Get Started
I Concentrate On You
I Cover The Waterfront
I Love You
I Loves You Porgy

I Only Have Eyes For You
I'm A Fool To Want You
Indian Summer
It Ain't Necessarily So
It Never Entered My Mind
It's You Or No One
Just One Of Those Things
Love For Sale
Lover, Come Back To Me
The Man I Love
Mr. Lucky
My Funny Valentine
My Heart Stood Still
My Man's Gone Now

Old Folks
On A Clear Day
Our Love Is Here To Stay
'Round Midnight
Secret Love
September In The Rain
Serenade In Blue
Shiny Stockings
Since I Fell For You
So In Love
So Nice (Summer Samba)
Some Other Time
Stormy Weather
The Summer Knows

Summer Night
Summertime
Teach Me Tonight
That Sunday, That Summer
The Girl From Ipanema
Then I'll Be Tired Of You
There's No You
Time On My Hands
'Tis Autumn
Where Or When
Who Cares?
With A Song In My Heart
You Go To My Head
And Hundreds More!

The New Real Book - Volume 1 (C, Bb or Eb)

Angel Eyes
Anthropology
Autumn Leaves
Beautiful Love
Bernie's Tune
Blue Bossa
Blue Daniel
But Beautiful
Chain Of Fools
Chelsea Bridge
Compared To What
Darn That Dream
Desafinado
Early Autumn

Eighty One
E.S.P.
Everything Happens To Me
Feel Like Makin' Love
Footprints
Four
Four On Six
Gee Baby Ain't I Good
To You
Gone With The Wind
Here's That Rainy Day
I Love Lucy
I Mean You
I Should Care

I Thought About You
If I Were A Bell
Imagination
The Island
Jersey Bounce
Joshua
Lady Bird
Like Someone In Love
Little Sunflower
Lush Life
Mercy, Mercy, Mercy
The Midnight Sun
Monk's Mood
Moonlight In Vermont

My Shining Hour
Nature Boy
Nefertiti
Nothing Personal
Oleo
Once I Loved
Out Of This World
Pent Up House
Portrait Of Tracy
Put It Where You Want It
Robbin's Nest
Ruby, My Dear
Satin Doll
Search For Peace

Shaker Song
Skylark
A Sleepin' Bee
Solar
Speak No Evil
St. Thomas
Street Life
Tenderly
These Foolish Things
This Masquerade
Three Views Of A Secret
Waltz For Debby
Willow Weep For Me
And Many More!

The New Real Book Play-Along CDs (For Volume 1)

CD #1 - Jazz Classics - Lady Bird, Bouncin' With Bud, Up Jumped Spring, Monk's Mood, Doors, Very Early, Eighty One, Voyage **& More!**

CD #2 - Choice Standards - Beautiful Love, Darn That Dream, Moonlight In Vermont, Trieste, My Shining Hour, I Should Care **& More!**

CD #3 - Pop-Fusion - Morning Dance, Nothing Personal, La Samba, Hideaway, This Masquerade, Three Views Of A Secret, Rio **& More!**

World-Class Rhythm Sections, featuring Mark Levine, Larry Dunlap, Sky Evergreen, Bob Magnusson, Keith Jones, Vince Lateano & Tom Hayashi

The New Real Book - Volume 2 (C, Bb or Eb)

Afro-Centric
After You've Gone
Along Came Betty
Bessie's Blues
Black Coffee
Blues For Alice
Body And Soul
Bolivia
The Boy Next Door
Bye Bye Blackbird
Cherokee
A Child Is Born
Cold Duck Time
Day By Day

Django
Equinox
Exactly Like You
Falling Grace
Five Hundred Miles High
Freedom Jazz Dance
Giant Steps
Harlem Nocturne
Hi-Fly
Honeysuckle Rose
I Hadn't Anyone 'Til You
I'll Be Around
I'll Get By
Ill Wind

I'm Glad There Is You
Impressions
In Your Own Sweet Way
It's The Talk Of The Town
Jordu
Killer Joe
Lullaby Of The Leaves
Manha De Carneval
The Masquerade Is Over
Memories Of You
Moment's Notice
Mood Indigo
My Ship
Naima

Nica's Dream
Once In A While
Perdido
Rosetta
Sea Journey
Senor Blues
September Song
Seven Steps To Heaven
Silver's Serenade
So Many Stars
Some Other Blues
Song For My Father
Sophisticated Lady
Spain

Stablemates
Stardust
Sweet And Lovely
That's All
There Is No Greater Love
'Til There Was You
Time Remembered
Turn Out The Stars
Unforgettable
While We're Young
Whisper Not
Will You Still Be Mine?
You're Everything
And Many More!

The New Real Book - Volume 3 (C, Bb, Eb or Bass clef)

Actual Proof
Ain't That Peculiar
Almost Like Being In Love
Another Star
Autumn Serenade
Bird Of Beauty
Black Nile
Blue Moon
Butterfly
Caravan
Ceora
Close Your Eyes
Creepin'
Day Dream

Dolphin Dance
Don't Be That Way
Don't Blame Me
Emily
Everything I Have Is Yours
For All We Know
Freedomland
The Gentle Rain
Get Ready
A Ghost Of A Chance
Heat Wave
How Sweet It Is
I Fall In Love Too Easily
I Got It Bad

I Hear A Rhapsody
If You Could See Me Now
In A Mellow Tone
In A Sentimental Mood
Inner Urge
Invitation
The Jitterbug Waltz
Just Friends
Just You, Just Me
Knock On Wood
The Lamp Is Low
Laura
Let's Stay Together
Lonely Woman

Maiden Voyage
Moon And Sand
Moonglow
My Girl
On Green Dolphin Street
Over The Rainbow
Prelude To A Kiss
Respect
Ruby
The Second Time Around
Serenata
The Shadow Of Your Smile
So Near, So Far
Solitude

Speak Like A Child
Spring Is Here
Stairway To The Stars
Star Eyes
Stars Fell On Alabama
Stompin' At The Savoy
Sweet Lorraine
Taking A Chance On Love
This Is New
Too High
(Used To Be A) Cha Cha
When Lights Are Low
You Must Believe In Spring
And Many More!

The All Jazz Real Book

Over 540 pages of tunes as recorded by:
Miles, Trane, Bill Evans, Cannonball, Scofield, Brecker, Yellowjackets, Bird, Mulgrew Miller, Kenny Werner, MJQ, McCoy Tyner, Kurt Elling, Brad Mehldau, Don Grolnick, Kenny Garrett, Patitucci, Jerry Bergonzi, Stanley Clarke, Tom Harrell, Herbie Hancock, Horace Silver, Stan Getz, Sonny Rollins, and MORE!

Includes a free CD of many of the melodies
(featuring Bob Sheppard & Friends.). $44 list price.
Available in C, Bb, Eb

The European Real Book

An amazing collection of some of the greatest jazz compositions ever recorded! Available in C, Bb and Eb. $40

- Over 100 of Europe's best jazz writers.
- 100% accurate, composer-approved charts.
- 400 pages of fresh, exciting sounds from virtually every country in Europe.
- Sher Music's superior legibility and signature calligraphy makes reading the music easy.

Listen to FREE MP3 FILES of many of the songs at www.shermusic.com!

See **www.shermusic.com** for more information, including a complete list of tunes in all our fake books.
To order, call (800) 444-7437 or fax (707) 763-2038

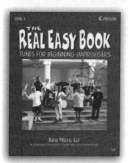

The Real Easy Book Vol. 1
TUNES FOR BEGINNING IMPROVISERS

Published by Sher Music Co. in conjunction with the Stanford Jazz Workshop. $22 list price.

The easiest tunes from Horace Silver, Eddie Harris, Freddie Hubbard, Red Garland, Sonny Rollins, Cedar Walton, Wes Montgomery Cannonball Adderly, etc. Get yourself or your beginning jazz combo sounding good right away with the first fake book ever designed for the beginning improviser.
Available in C, Bb, Eb and Bass Clef.

The Real Easy Book Vol. 2
TUNES FOR INTERMEDIATE IMPROVISERS

Published by Sher Music Co. in conjunction with the Stanford Jazz Workshop. Over 240 pages. $29.

The best intermediate-level tunes by: Charlie Parker, John Coltrane, Miles Davis, John Scofield, Sonny Rollins, Horace Silver, Wes Montgomery, Freddie Hubbard, Cal Tjader, Cannonball Adderly, and more!
Both volumes feature instructional material tailored for each tune. Perfect for jazz combos!
Available in C, Bb, Eb and Bass Clef.

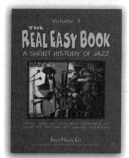

The Real Easy Book Vol. 3
A SHORT HISTORY OF JAZZ

Published by Sher Music Co. in conjunction with the Stanford Jazz Workshop. Over 200 pages. $25.

History text and tunes from all eras and styles of jazz. Perfect for classroom use. Available in C, Bb, Eb and Bass Clef versions.

The Best of Sher Music Co. Real Books
100+ TUNES YOU NEED TO KNOW

A collection of the best-known songs from the world leader in jazz fake books – Sher Music Co.!

Includes songs by: Miles Davis, John Coltrane, Bill Evans, Duke Ellington, Antonio Carlos Jobim, Charlie Parker, John Scofield, Michael Brecker, Weather Report, Horace Silver, Freddie Hubbard, Thelonious Monk, Cannonball Adderley, and many more!
$26. Available in C, Bb, Eb and Bass Clef.

The Serious Jazz Book II
THE HARMONIC APPROACH

By Barry Finnerty, Endorsed by: Joe Lovano, Jamey Aebersold, Hubert Laws, Mark Levine, etc.

- A 200 page, exhaustive study of how to master the harmonic content of songs.
- Contains explanations of every possible type of chord that is used in jazz.
- Clear musical examples to help achieve real harmonic control over melodic improvisation.
- For any instrument. $32. Money back gurantee!

The Serious Jazz Practice Book By Barry Finnerty

A unique and comprehensive plan for mastering the basic building blocks of the jazz language. It takes the most widely-used scales and chords and gives you step-by-step exercises that dissect them into hundreds of cool, useable patterns.
Includes CD - $30 list price.

"The book I've been waiting for!" – Randy Brecker.

"The best book of intervallic studies I've ever seen."
– Mark Levine

The Jazz Theory Book

By Mark Levine, the most comprehensive Jazz Theory book ever published! $38 list price.
- Over 500 pages of text and over 750 musical examples.
- Written in the language of the working jazz musician, this book is easy to read and user-friendly. At the same time, it is the most comprehensive study of jazz harmony and theory ever published.
- Mark Levine has worked with Bobby Hutcherson, Cal Tjader, Joe Henderson, Woody Shaw, and many other jazz greats.

Jazz Piano Masterclass With Mark Levine
"THE DROP 2 BOOK"

The long-awaited book from the author of "The Jazz Piano Book!" A complete study on how to use "drop 2" chord voicings to create jazz piano magic! 68 pages, plus CD of Mark demonstrating each exercise. $19 list.

"Will make you sound like a real jazz piano player in no time." – Jamey Aebersold

Metaphors For The Musician
By Randy Halberstadt

This practical and enlightening book will help any jazz player or vocalist look at music with "new eyes." Designed for any level of player, on any instrument, "Metaphors For The Musician" provides numerous exercises throughout to help the reader turn these concepts into musical reality.

Guaranteed to help you improve your musicianship. 330 pages – $29 list price. Satisfaction guaranteed!

The Jazz Musicians Guide To Creative Practicing
By David Berkman

Finally a book to help musicians use their practice time wisely! Covers tune analysis, breaking hard tunes into easy components, how to swing better, tricks to playing fast bebop lines, and much more! 150+pages, plus CD. $29 list.

"Fun to read and bursting with things to do and ponder." – Bob Mintzer

The 'Real Easy' Ear Training Book
By Roberta Radley

For all musicians, regardless of instrument or experience, this is the most comprehensive book on "hearing the changes" ever published!
- Covers both beginning and intermediate ear training exercises.
- Music Teachers: You will find this book invaluable in teaching ear training to your students.

Book includes 168 pages of instructional text and musical examples, plus two CDs! $29 list price.

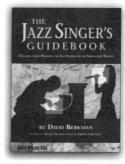

The Jazz Singer's Guidebook By David Berkman
A COURSE IN JAZZ HARMONY AND SCAT SINGING FOR THE SERIOUS JAZZ VOCALIST

A clear, step-by-step approach for serious singers who want to improve their grasp of jazz harmony and gain a deeper understanding of music fundamentals.

This book will change how you hear music and make you a better singer, as well as give you the tools to develop your singing in directions you may not have thought possible.

$26 – includes audio CD demonstrating many exercises.

LATIN MUSIC BOOKS, CDs, DVD

The Latin Real Book (C, Bb or Eb)
The only professional-level Latin fake book ever published!

Ray Barretto	Arsenio Rodriguez	Manny Oquendo	Ivan Lins
Eddie Palmieri	Tito Rodriguez	Puerto Rico All-Stars	Djavan
Fania All-Stars	Orquesta Aragon	Issac Delgaldo	Tom Jobim
Tito Puente	Beny Moré	Ft. Apache Band	Toninho Horta
Ruben Blades	Cal Tjader	Dave Valentin	Joao Bosco
Los Van Van	Andy Narell	Paquito D'Rivera	Milton Nascimento
NG La Banda	Mario Bauza	Clare Fischer	Leila Pinheiro
Irakere	Dizzy Gilllespie	Chick Corea	Gal Costa
Celia Cruz	Mongo Santamaria	Sergio Mendes	**And Many More!**

The Latin Real Book Sampler CD

12 of the greatest Latin Real Book tunes as played by the original artists: Tito Puente, Ray Barretto, Andy Narell, Puerto Rico Allstars, Bacacoto, etc.

$16 list price. Available in U.S.A. only.

The Conga Drummer's Guidebook By Michael Spiro

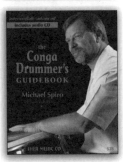

Includes CD - $28 list price. The only method book specifically designed for the intermediate to advanced conga drummer. It goes behind the superficial licks and explains how to approach any Afro-Latin rhythm with the right feel, so you can create a groove like the pros!.

"This book is awesome. Michael is completely knowledgable about his subject."   – Dave Garibaldi

"A breakthrough book for all students of the conga drum."
– Karl Perazzo

Introduction to the Conga Drum - DVD
By Michael Spiro

For beginners, or anyone needing a solid foundation in conga drum technique.

Jorge Alabe – "Mike Spiro is a great conga teacher. People can learn real conga technique from this DVD."

John Santos – "A great musician/teacher who's earned his stripes"

1 hour, 55 minutes running time. $25.

Muy Caliente!

Afro-Cuban Play-Along CD and Book
Rebeca Mauleón - Keyboard
Oscar Stagnaro - Bass
Orestes Vilató - Timbales
Carlos Caro - Bongos
Edgardo Cambon - Congas
Over 70 min. of smokin' Latin grooves!
Stereo separation so you can eliminate the bass or piano. Play-along with a rhythm section featuring some of the top Afro-Cuban musicians in the world! $18.

The True Cuban Bass

By Carlos Del Puerto, (bassist with Irakere) and **Silvio Vergara,** $22.

For acoustic or electric bass; English and Spanish text; Includes CDs of either historic Cuban recordings or Carlos playing each exercise; Many transcriptions of complete bass parts for tunes in different Cuban styles – the roots of Salsa.

101 Montunos
By Rebeca Mauleón

The only comprehensive study of Latin piano playing ever published.

- Bi-lingual text (English/Spanish)
- 2 CDs of the author demonstrating each montuno
- Covers over 100 years of Afro-Cuban styles, including the danzón, guaracha, mambo, merengue and songo—from Peruchin to Eddie Palmieri. $28

The Salsa Guide Book
By Rebeca Mauleón

The only complete method book on salsa ever published! 260 pages. $25.

Carlos Santana – "A true treasure of knowledge and information about Afro-Cuban music."
Mark Levine, author of The Jazz Piano Book. – "This is the book on salsa."
Sonny Bravo, pianist with Tito Puente – "This will be the salsa 'bible' for years to come."
Oscar Hernández, pianist with Rubén Blades – "An excellent and much needed resource."

The Brazilian Guitar Book

By Nelson Faria, one of Brazil's best new guitarists.

- Over 140 pages of comping patterns, transcriptions and chord melodies for samba, bossa, baião, etc.
- Complete chord voicings written out for each example.
- Comes with a CD of Nelson playing each example.
- The most complete Brazilian guitar method ever published! $28.

Joe Diorio – "Nelson Faria's book is a welcome addition to the guitar literature. I'm sure those who work with this volume will benefit greatly"

Inside The Brazilian Rhythm Section
By Nelson Faria and Cliff Korman

This is the first book/CD package ever published that provides an opportunity for bassists, guitarists, pianists and drummers to interact and play-along with a master Brazilian rhythm section. Perfect for practicing both accompanying and soloing.

$28 list price for book and 2 CDs - including the charts for the CD tracks and sample parts for each instrument, transcribed from the recording.

The Latin Bass Book
A PRACTICAL GUIDE
By Oscar Stagnaro

The only comprehensive book ever published on how to play bass in authentic Afro-Cuban, Brazilian, Caribbean, Latin Jazz & South American styles. $34.

Over 250 pages of transcriptions of Oscar Stagnaro playing each exercise. Learn from the best!

Includes: 3 Play-Along CDs to accompany each exercise, featuring world-class rhythm sections.

Afro-Caribbean Grooves for Drumset

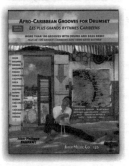

By Jean-Philippe Fanfant, drummer with Andy narell's band, Sakesho.

Covers grooves from 10 Caribbean nations, arranged for drumset.

Endorsed by Peter Erskine, Horacio Hernandez, etc.

CD includes both audio and video files. $25.

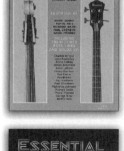
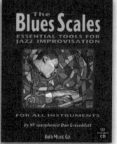